AF880198

Bolivia's Answer to Poverty, Economic Crisis, and Adjustment

The Emergency Social Fund

WORLD BANK

REGIONAL AND

SECTORAL STUDIES

Bolivia's Answer to Poverty, Economic Crisis, and Adjustment

The Emergency Social Fund

EDITED BY

STEEN JORGENSEN,

MARGARET GROSH,

AND

MARK SCHACTER

The World Bank
Washington, D.C.

© 1992 The International Bank for Reconstruction
and Development / The World Bank
1818 H Street, N.W., Washington, D.C. 20433

All rights reserved
Manufactured in the United States of America
First printing April 1992

The World Bank Regional and Sectoral Studies series provides an outlet for work that is relatively limited in its subject matter or geographical coverage but that contributes to the intellectual foundations of development operations and policy formulation. These studies have not necessarily been edited with the same rigor as Bank publications that carry the imprint of a university press.

The findings, interpretations, and conclusions expressed in this publication are those of the authors and should not be attributed in any manner to the World Bank, to its affiliated organizations, or to the members of its Board of Executive Directors or the countries they represent.

The material in this publication is copyrighted. Requests for permission to reproduce portions of it should be sent to the Office of the Publisher at the address shown in the copyright notice above. The World Bank encourages dissemination of its work and will normally give permission promptly and, when the reproduction is for noncommercial purposes, without asking a fee. Permission to copy portions for classroom use is granted through the Copyright Clearance Center, 27 Congress Street, Salem, Massachusetts 01970, U.S.A.

The complete backlist of publications from the World Bank is shown in the annual *Index of Publications*, which contains an alphabetical title list and indexes of subjects, authors, and countries and regions. The latest edition is available free of charge from Distribution Unit, Office of the Publisher, The World Bank, 1818 H Street, N.W., Washington, D.C. 20433, U.S.A., or from Publications, The World Bank, 66, avenue d'Iéna, 75116 Paris, France.

Cover design by Sam Ferro

Library of Congress Cataloging-in-Publication Data

Bolivia's answer to poverty, economic crisis, and adjustment : the
Emergency Social Fund / edited by Steen Jorgensen, Margaret Grosh,
and Mark Schacter.
p. cm.—(World Bank regional and sectoral studies)
Includes bibliographical references.
ISBN 0-8213-2056-4
1. Fondo Social de Emergencia (Bolivia) 2. Public welfare—
Bolivia. 3. Poor—Government policy—Bolivia. I. Jorgensen,
Steen, 1958– . II. Grosh, Margaret E. III. Schacter, Mark, 1957–
. IV. Series.
HV188.B65 1992
362.5'82'0984—dc20 92-8591
CIP

Contents

Reader's Guide

This collection brings together material on the Bolivian Emergency Social Fund (ESF) in response to a steady stream of requests for information about the agency's experience. The collection is structured so that the reader may read only selected chapters. The purpose of this guide is to help the reader decide which chapters correspond to his or her particular interest.

The collection is divided into five main parts. Part I (Chapters 1 and 2) presents introductory material and the story of the ESF. Part II (Chapters 3 and 4) contains a review of the many evaluations of the ESF, and a study of the impact of ESF employment. Part III (Chapters 5 through 7) presents three issues brought up by the ESF experience, namely, procurement, collaboration with non-governmental organizations, and responding to local demands. Part IV (Chapters 8 and 9) looks at the options after the ESF, including a look at its successor. Part V (Chapters 10 and 11) contains a summary of achievements, and recommendations for replication. Because of its nature as a collection of separate papers, there is some overlap between chapters.

PART I

Chapter 1 is a primer on the ESF, containing a concise description of its structure, operational procedures, mandate, material achievements and the economic conditions in Bolivia that led to its establishment. Those who are well familiar with the ESF may wish to skip this chapter. Other readers will find it a useful introduction, and a source of important background information that will give context and meaning to the other papers in this volume.

Chapter 2 takes the reader back to 1986, when the possibility of creating what was to become the ESF was beginning to be discussed by a small group of Bolivians and World Bank staff members. The proposal challenged Bank orthodoxy in key areas such as procurement and the value of "job-creation" schemes. The chapter reflects some early discussions of targeting, the need to focus on retrenched public sector employees, social assistance versus employment, and institutional arrangements.

PART II

The considerable body of formal evaluation material that has been written on the ESF over the past four years is surveyed in Chapter 3. The review covers the ESF's administrative efficiency, and the effectiveness of its targeting, as well as its impact on the labor market, public investment, the overall Bolivian economy, and the local institutions with which it worked. The conclusion of the chapter summarizes, very briefly, the main lessons learned.

Chapter 4 presents an evaluation of the impact of the ESF on workers employed in ESF-funded projects. Several findings are presented, including that ESF workers were poorer than average, and that the ESF generated substantial temporary gains in earnings for workers over what they would have earned without the program.

PART III

The ESF's unconventional procurement practices are analyzed in Chapter 5. While procurement practices violated many tenets of the World Bank's orthodoxy on procurement, they were nevertheless well suited to the ESF's mandate and to Bolivian conditions.

One of the ESF's accomplishments was its ability to work with non-governmental organizations (NGOs). Chapter 6 describes the ESF's experience with these groups, suggesting that there are both risks and advantages in attempts at close cooperation between a central funding agency and NGOs. NGOs tended to fare better when they used ESF funding to consolidate existing programs rather than to expand them or create new ones. While NGOs can be extremely useful intermediaries for extending benefits to the poor, particularly in the social sectors, they cannot always be counted on to reach the poorest of the poor.

Chapter 7 is an economic analysis of the central problem inherent in a demand-driven fund like the ESF: establishing a balance between the preferences of the groups seeking funding and the priorities of the central funding agency. This theoretical analysis is illustrated by examples from the ESF. Recommendations include imposing counterpart fund requirements, comparing projects within a category and not among categories, and introducing new administrative performance criteria.

PART IV

Following up on a success story is always hard, and the temptation is strong to continue along the same lines. Chapter 8 presents the various options the Bolivian government faced when trying to decide what to do after the ESF was scheduled to go out of business. These included continuing with the ESF, moving all activities back to the line ministries, and establishing a new permanent institution with similar characteristics to the ESF.

The actual path taken to resolve the continuity problem is presented in Chapter 9. This chapter discusses the transition from the ESF's short-term, emergency mandate to the longer-run development focus of its successor organization, the Social Investment Fund. The chapter focuses on changes in targeting and institutional set-up.

PART V

Many other countries are looking to replicate the ESF experience. Chapter 10 assesses the conditions under which it would be relevant to establish an institution like the ESF. Important conditions to consider should be the goal of the institution, whether to provide employment or to use an alternative tool such as commodity or service subsidies or commodity distribution to accomplish the delineated goal and, if employment is chosen as the tool, the institutional structure for the employment scheme. The chapter counsels against a "carbon-copy" approach in other countries.

Chapter 11 briefly summarizes the successes and shortcomings of the ESF and the key ingredients of its success. It provides references to the other chapters where further discussions can be found.

1

What? Why? How? A Primer on the ESF

by Mark Schacter, Margaret Grosh, and Steen Jorgensen

The Emergency Social Fund (ESF) was created by the government of Bolivia in December 1986 to alleviate the social cost of a crisis brought on by poor macroeconomic policies, and to protect the poor during implementation of a macroeconomic stabilization and adjustment program begun in late 1985. The World Bank and other multilateral and bilateral agencies financed the ESF. For the World Bank, this was its first project dedicated specifically to protecting the poor during a macroeconomic adjustment program.

The ESF was designed as a quick-disbursing mechanism for financing small, technically simple projects formulated and requested by a variety of public, private and voluntary agencies. In appraising project proposals, the ESF focused on two key criteria: (a) was the project likely to benefit the poor? and (b) was the project technically sound? Projects were carried out by private contractors or nongovernmental organizations (NGOs), and supervised by a third party with the necessary technical qualifications.

The following data, compiled on April 30, 1990, provide a recent "snapshot" of the ESF. A total of 3,045 projects, valued at $181.1 million had been approved; $80.9 million (45 percent) was directed to social infrastructure projects such as the construction and repair of schools, health clinics, and small water and sewerage systems; $76.2 million (42 percent) to economic infrastructure projects such as road upgrading, irrigation, drainage, and reforestation; $17.1 million (9 percent) to social assistance, i.e., the provision of services in health, nutrition and education; and $6.9 million (4 percent) to cooperatives and small credit projects.[1]

There were 1,133 projects worth $69.8 million that were in the course of being implemented; 1,689 projects valued at $100.5 million had been completed. The amount of project funding actually disbursed by the ESF totalled $133.7 million; the ESF's own administrative expenses amounted to $6.5 million, or 3.6 percent of the value of its project portfolio.

The average cost per person-month of employment generated was $200 for economic infrastructure projects, $284 for social infrastructure projects, and $512 for production support projects.

There were 18,915 persons employed at ESF-financed projects; to date, 383,462 person-months of employment have been created. A partial summary of particular achievements is shown in Table 1.1.

In contrast to the snapshot of a full portfolio, Table 1.2 provides a picture of the dramatic growth of the ESF's portfolio and accomplishments over time.

Background

The Economic Background and the Adjustment Program

The Bolivian economy entered a steep decline in 1980, tumbling to near collapse five years later. The economic bust followed abruptly on the boom years of the 1970s when external capital poured into Bolivia in the wake of discoveries of substantial oil and gas resources. Bolivia's economic performance deteriorated rapidly around 1980. At the same time the flow of foreign financing dried up and net foreign transfers became strongly negative. GDP fell steadily, capital flight accel-

Table 1.1 The ESF's Material Achievements—A Snapshot

Social Infrastructure	
181,038	meters of sewerage and water systems installed
7,084	low income houses
259	health posts
224	schools
Economic Infrastructure	
2,760	blocks of urban streets paved
6,368	kilometers of inter-city roads improved
30,775	meters of irrigation works constructed
Social Assistance	
4,426,137	meals (including school breakfasts)
640,000	school text books provided
65,335	school desks built
27,951	persons graduated from training programs

Source: ESF.

Table 1.2 The ESF's Achievements Over Time

	Projects Approved	
Year End	*Number (cumulative)*	*Value (million $)*
1987	436	36.5
1988	1,652	114.9
1989	2,797	161.7
	Projects Completed	
Year End	*Number (cumulative)*	*Value (million $)*
1987	45	1.2
1988	429	22.9
1989	1,268	78.2
Month	*Persons Employed at ESF Projects (non-cumulative)*	
6/1987	3,137	
9/1987	5,334	
12/1987	9,187	
3/1988	11,926	
6/1988	13,913	
9/1988	20,029	
12/1988	25,919	
3/1989	28,470	
6/1989	29,338	
9/1989	21,200	
12/1989	19,200	

Source: ESF.

erated and economic policies became erratic and inconsistent. Hyperinflation ensued, the annual rate of price increase averaging 24,000 percent over the one-year period leading up to September 1985. By this time, per capita GDP had fallen by more than a fifth since 1980, public sector deficits had climbed to about one quarter of GDP, shortages were widespread and popular discontent was threatening the peace of La Paz and other major cities.

The government of President Paz Estenssoro, which took office in August 1985, acted quickly and decisively on the economic front. It set in motion a comprehensive stabilization and structural adjustment program whose main goals were to cut inflation, restore external and internal financial equilibrium, and lay the foundations for sustained economic recovery and growth. The new economic program included the freeing of most prices, deregulation of external trade and the labor market, establishment of a uniform exchange rate, cutting of the public sector deficit, and a reform of the tax system with a view to improving public finance in the long term. The program gained support from the International Monetary Fund (IMF) and the World Bank in 1986.

The program had a dramatic impact on the public sector. The government aimed to introduce a radically new view of the public sector, moving from the entrenched notion of a "paternalistic" state involved in all aspects of economic activity to the idea that its proper role was to provide basic public services and to be involved only in a limited way in the extraction and processing of natural resources. The most visible casualty of this approach was COMIBOL, the state-owned tin-mining concern. It was closed for restructuring, and about 77 percent (about 23,000) of its employees were fired. Other broad-brush reforms, affecting areas such as public sector salary policy and accounting and control systems, were also set in motion.

Bolivians felt positive effects of the stabilization program almost immediately. Inflation fell to 11 percent in 1987, and settled around 21 percent in the two following years. In addition, public sector deficits were brought under control, and the exchange rate remained unified. Growth, however, has taken longer to occur. Although economic decline was halted, expansion was painfully slow in the latter half of the 1980s, and continued to be so into 1990.

Effect of the Economic Crisis on the Poor

While data are sketchy, there is certainly reason to assume that the poor suffered relatively more than other groups during the 1980-1985 crisis. The crisis and hyperinflation created an environment where those most fit to survive economically were those who had access to information and political power. Because the poor had neither, they tended to lose out in the sharp competition to maintain living standards in the face of the economy's steep decline.

The government's economic policies during the crisis probably hurt the poor. The distribution and financing of state subsidies were structured in such a way that the poor could rarely benefit.[2] For example, the provision of credit to farmers heavily favored large landowners, while little was made available to peasant farmers. In addition, public sector spending on programs to benefit the rural poor, including agricultural extension services, health services and education (particularly basic education) fell sharply in real terms during the crisis.

The spiraling inflation experienced during the crisis also had a devastating impact on the purchasing power and wealth of many poor Bolivians. The better off were able to protect the real value of their incomes and assets from inflation (through speculative dealings, land ownership, foreign bank accounts, etc.). Indeed, it appears that one result of Bolivia's economic crisis was that there was a marked shift in income distribution toward the wealthier end of the spectrum. Real incomes in urban areas of the country dropped by 60 percent between 1980 and 1985, while the share of Bolivia's total urban income accounted for by the wealthiest 5 percent of the population doubled.

Social Conditions

By the mid-1980s, social indicators in Bolivia were (and remain today) the worst in South America. Bolivia's per capita GNP of $570 made its population the poorest on the continent. Infant mortality was twice the average for the region, at 110 per 1,000 live births; the rate reached 277 per 1,000 in some of the poorest areas. Diarrhea-parasitic and acute respiratory infections were the most common causes of infant and child deaths. The maternal mortality rate, 48 per 10,000 live births, was the highest in the hemisphere. Tuberculosis was a prominent health problem, and tropical ailments such as malaria and Chagas' disease were widespread. Malnutrition was pervasive: the majority of the population lived in families whose income was insufficient to cover minimal daily food requirements.

Domestic sanitation was poor. Only about 69 percent of the urban population and 10 percent of the rural population had access to piped water (which was often unpotable); in Bolivia's four major cities, 65 percent of the population had no facilities for excreta disposal, and such facilities were virtually non-existent in rural areas.

The coverage of education has become less of a concern than it once was, but serious problems remain. On the one hand, the literacy rate almost doubled from 32 percent in 1950 to 63 percent in 1985, a phenomenon linked to a dramatic expansion in access to education. However, dropout and repetition rates remained high, and classroom conditions remained poor: up to 90 percent of students in rural areas and up to half of all urban students still did not have textbooks.

The Emergency Social Fund

The Concept

The primary motivating factor behind the creation of the ESF was that Bolivia was poorly equipped, institutionally, to deal with the social costs of its economic crisis; nor could its public agencies be expected to cope with any additional social costs that might flow from the adjustment program. The three central ministries responsible for social welfare—Health, Education, and Housing and Urban Development—lacked sufficient skilled manpower, financial resources and management capacity to mount an effective response.

Given the necessity for reduced public sector spending entailed by the adjustment program, the ESF was intended to be dependent almost entirely on external loans and grants. Start-up funding was provided by the Bolivian government and the United Nations Development Program (UNDP) became involved at an early stage. The World Bank was the ESF's first major external donor; later, as the ESF proved its ability to perform, it received additional support from a variety of foreign and multilateral donors.

The ESF was designed as a temporary institution, scheduled to be terminated at the end of 1989. It was hoped that three years would be sufficient time for the economy to recover to the point where the government could ease austerity measures and build increases in social and infrastructure spending into the regular budget, thereby rendering the ESF unnecessary. Later, the ESF's life was extended by 15 months to the end of March 1991, to allow for an orderly transfer of its experience to the relevant permanent government agencies.

From the outset, the ESF generated a mixture of interest and skepticism at the World Bank: interest because it marked the Bank's first intervention aimed directly at easing the social costs of adjustment, an area where the Bank had been strongly criticized for being too slow to act; skepticism because employment generation was the main purpose of the ESF, and Bank staff generally frowned upon supporting "job-creation" schemes (see Chapter 2).

The ESF was to fund, with the shortest lead-time feasible, relatively small and technically simple projects that were to be proposed, designed and carried out by national, regional and local organizations in the public, private and voluntary sectors. Four types of projects were considered suitable for ESF funding: (a) economic infrastructure—infrastructure closely related to productive activities, such as road upgrading, urban improvement, irrigation, flood control and reforestation; (b) social infrastructure—infrastructure for health and education, water and sanitation, and basic housing; (c) social assistance—recurrent costs in education and training, vaccinations, school breakfasts, and production of school materials; and (d) production support—credit provided through NGOs to microenterprises producing in the informal sector and to cooperatives in mining and agriculture. Initially, at least, the ESF's designers intended that funding would be concentrated on labor-intensive projects that would create employment opportunities for the poor while also providing services and infrastructure to poor communities, thereby aiding in their economic development.

While the ESF evolved considerably over its four-year life, certain characteristics remained fundamental and unchanging:

First, the ESF was *demand-driven*. In other words, the portfolio of projects carried by the ESF was determined by the requests it received for funding from organizations throughout the country. The decision to make the ESF a demand-driven institution was based on both ideological and operational considerations. The adjustment program's ideological emphasis on dismantling the paternalistic state and strengthening initiative and self-sufficiency among the general population fit well with the concept of a demand-driven funding agency. Moreover, with the burden of proposing projects resting on the requesting organizations, the ESF could remain a relatively small agency, able to respond to changing conditions with speed and flexibility. It was also believed that a demand-driven process would give requesting organizations a sense of "ownership" of their projects that would otherwise have been absent.

Second, the ESF was primarily a *financial intermediary*. Its main function was to fund, and then monitor, projects that met its criteria. Although it provided technical assistance where supervision and implementation were concerned, it did not act as an implementing agency. The rationale was much the same as that for making the ESF demand-driven: keep the ESF's bureaucratic apparatus as small as possible, enhance local capacity to invest in development, and foster a sense of "ownership" in projects.

Third, the ESF depended heavily on participation by organizations in the *private and voluntary sectors.* Functioning as contractors carrying out projects or as requesters of funds, private and voluntary groups (non-governmental organizations, for example) had an important role to play.

In order to give the ESF the capacity to operate swiftly and efficiently in the face of the prevailing economic crisis, the government placed it outside the normal bureaucratic structure. Its executive director reported directly to the president, who took a strong personal interest in its work and sheltered it from the most heavy-handed forms of political manipulation. Moreover, the ESF was exempted from several important public sector regulations. Its ability to disburse funds quickly to approved projects was made possible by its being permitted to avoid the complicated and slow procurement procedures imposed on other state agencies. As well, it was allowed to pay salaries to its staff that were considerably higher than those received by government employees, a concession that enabled it to attract a highly qualified group of professionals.

It is worth noting that the ESF went through several conceptual incarnations before the final design was realized in late 1986. Earlier discussions in 1985 focused on more traditional approaches to poverty alleviation such as distribution of food and medicines or provision of subsidies for selected items. These proposals were dismissed as being inconsistent with the reduced role for the state and the bias against paternalism embodied in the adjustment program. Moreover, subsidy or distribution programs were judged likely to entail substantial administrative costs and were regarded as being opposed to the goals of more efficient resource allocation that were central to the government's new economic policies.

Operational Issues

Targeting. It was decided early in the life of the ESF that any attempt to finely target project benefits to the poorest segments of the population would be unduly time-consuming and expensive. Accordingly, the ESF settled on rough-and-ready targeting methods. Targeting tended to be assessed on a project-by-project basis. ESF appraisal staff would travel to the site of a proposed project and determine, on the spot, whether by virtue either of its location (e.g., a poor neighborhood) or of the benefits it would provide (e.g., primary health care) the project was likely to serve or attract mainly poor people. More broadly, the ESF established funding targets for each of the four project types and each of the country's nine departments. (Departments are Bolivia's main administrative units.) Funding goals were based on the proportion of national population in each department, and were adjusted for departmental income per capita, unemployment, infant mortality and school attendance, among other factors. (For a more detailed discussion of targeting in the ESF, see Chapters 3 and 4.)

Evolution. The ESF evolved considerably over its life. Indeed, one of the things most evident to World Bank staff during their supervision of the ESF was that its managers often identified weaknesses and had taken corrective action before the Bank realized that there were problems. It was this capacity to respond, as much as its more tangible, material results, that has aroused interest in the ESF. The evolution of the ESF was manifested in changes in its portfolio of projects, in procedures, and in organization.

Project Portfolio. Early in its life, the ESF focused on funding, as quickly as possible, projects that created as much employment as possible. Consequently, a relatively large number of urban improvement projects, such as street paving, were undertaken because of their high employment content and simple technical nature. But as the ESF gained experience and confidence, and as the quality of its bank of project proposals improved, it began to adopt a longer-term, development perspective. Economic infrastructure projects in areas such as irrigation, road drainage and flood control began to receive higher priority.

There was also a relatively small number of social assistance projects being funded in the earliest stages of the ESF. Few proposals were submitted, and no strong effort was made by ESF staff to attract proposals in this sector. The latter was probably due to a mix of factors, including concerns about the complicated nature of these types of projects (it is a much less straightforward matter to assess a proposal for a nutrition program than for a road-paving project), the fact that the professional background of ESF staff was heavily weighted toward engineering and economics, and the fact that many NGOs, who would have been ideal sponsors for social assistance projects, were initially hesitant to become involved with the ESF. To increase the emphasis on social assistance, the ESF hired staff with expertise in the area, and created special social assistance units. These changes also had an effect on NGOs' attitudes, because they helped convince them that the ESF was indeed serious about funding social assistance projects.

The transition in focus at the ESF from a short-term, job-creation perspective to a longer-term, development outlook was seen in the shift that occurred in appraisal criteria applied to project proposals. Issues like sustainability, cost recovery and long-term social benefits gained importance, tilting the balance away from the earlier preoccupation with concerns about quick implementation and cost per employee-month generated.

Procedures. Two procedural advances were of considerable importance. The first was the development of the unit cost system (discussed below and in Chapter 5), upon which the ESF based its unique and effective system of procurement. The system took over a year to set up, and was built on the body of experience — successes and mistakes — accumulated by the appraisal staff during the start-up period of the ESF. The relative sophistication of the unit cost system was a striking contrast to the rudimentary appraisal practices used during the ESF's first months, when staff would sometimes do little more than make a quick "eyeball" estimate of the cost of a project, based on their observations from a site visit. While this was in keeping with the ESF's urgent need to get a large number of approved projects into the pipeline, it was also recognized that more precise (but still simple) techniques would have to be devised.

Another important development concerned the supervision of projects. As the portfolio of the ESF's projects expanded, it became apparent that there were serious problems with supervision and hence with the quality of work. Many supervising agencies proved to be quite unsophisticated, inexperienced and unreliable. At several projects, the supervising agency never appeared at the site, increasing the responsibility of the contractor. But the contractors themselves were, in many cases, small and inexperienced, relying to a high degree on sub-contractors. Moreover, the ESF's regional supervisors (zone chiefs) sometimes lacked a detailed understanding of the technical intricacies of the projects they were charged with monitoring.

The ESF responded by hiring technical specialists to support the zone chiefs. It also began subsidizing some supervising agencies to enable them to free up more staff to supervise projects and to pay travel expenses to remote project sites. These measures brought the quality problem under better control. (For a further discussion, see Chapter 3.)

Organization. By the middle of its first year of operation, the ESF was faced with a critical problem: it had attracted fewer project proposals than anticipated, and many of the proposals that it had received were too poorly formulated to be appraised. ESF staff concluded that too many local groups were: (a) unaware of the existence of the ESF, (b) doubtful that the ESF would actually fund their project proposals, or (c) technically incapable of submitting a properly formulated project proposal. This led to one of the first important organizational developments at the ESF: the establishment of the promotion department in September 1987 to foment more and better project proposals. (The function of the promotion department is described in the following section.)

Two later organizational developments were related to the evolution of the ESF's project portfolio. One development was the change in the mandate of the promotion department. While the promotion department's focus had originally been to encourage the submission of as large a number of technically sound project proposals as possible, by the end of 1988, mid-way through the ESF's four-year life, the department was redirected toward taking a more long-term, strategic approach. It became far more selective in the types of project proposals it would encourage, worrying less about short-term employment generation (though this always remained an important consideration) and more about the long-term impact and sustainability of projects. Promotion staff also became more deliberate about encouraging project proposals for particular sectors, such as social assistance, that had received less than their intended share of funding during the first two years of the ESF.

The second organizational change related to the evolution of the ESF's portfolio was the establishment of social assistance sub-units in the promotion, appraisal

Figure 1.1 Bolivia
Second Emergency Social Fund Project
E.S.F. Organization Chart

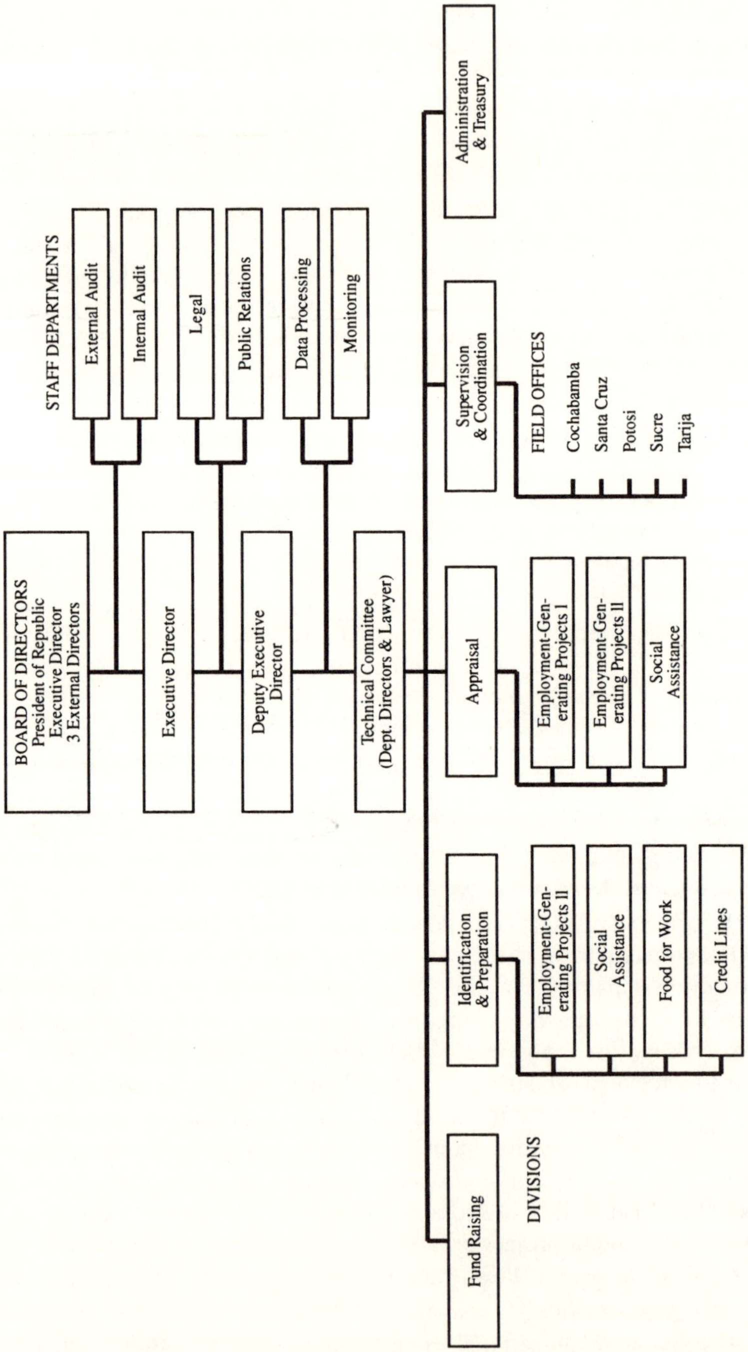

and supervision departments. This step was taken, again, as part of an attempt to put more funding into social assistance projects. It was felt within the ESF that part of the problem it was facing in the social assistance area — in attracting, appraising and supervising projects — was that the majority of its staff, being trained in disciplines such as engineering and economics, had little interest in, or understanding of, these types of projects. Accordingly, the new sub-unit was staffed with persons trained in relevant disciplines such as social work, psychology and education, and who had a strong interest in and aptitude for working with NGOs and community groups.

Another important organizational development was the creation of a free-standing technical auditing unit, which reported directly to the executive director of the ESF. The unit's job was to monitor continually the quality of works at ESF projects. This was one of the steps taken to correct the problem of poor quality of works, described above. The organizational chart of the ESF at maturity is shown in Figure 1.1.

Efficiency. At its peak, the ESF was approving, weekly, about 30 projects worth approximately $2 million. At certain periods, more than 1,000 projects were in the process of being implemented. This high level of activity was administered by a staff of fewer than 80 professionals; total staff, including support personnel, was about 130. (The ESF did not begin its operations with this level of staffing. The staff was increased gradually, as the ESF's workload increased.) As mentioned above, administrative costs accounted for about 3 percent of the ESF's budget. This level of efficiency was due to several factors: simple and standard appraisal and supervision procedures, clear lines of authority, high quality staff, excellent office technology, a good information system, etc. These are taken up in more detail in subsequent sections and chapters.

Management Information System. A key factor in the ESF's success in minimizing overhead was its microcomputer based management information system, which enabled ESF staff to call up data, (literally) at the push of a button, on the current status of any project, whether it be at the appraisal stage or in implementation. This capability was extremely important internally, from the point of view of controlling a geographically and sectorally diverse basket of projects, and externally, from the point of view of allowing donors to be shown precisely where their money was being spent.

The management information system consisted of several sub-systems. The first referred to the basic financial and administrative information for each project. Inter alia, it contained the project code, name, location, project type, requesting agency, contractor, supervisor, total project cost, cost financed by ESF, execution period, number of person-months of employment, number of direct and indirect beneficiaries, physical progress indicator, and disbursement information. The system was structured so that virtually any permutation of sub-project sorts, cross-tabs, or aggregations could be easily performed. A complete set of summary indicators was produced monthly and circulated internally in the ESF and to donor agencies and oversight authorities on request.

The ESF's financial accounts were thoroughly automated. Information on the financial history of each project was available. Aggregate information on the portfolio, on funds flowing in from the donor agencies, and disbursement projections based on various scenarios for project advance or flow of funds were available and used regularly in financial planning. Detailed accounts of each donor's funds were also included.

A second key component to the information system was the unit cost data base, discussed in more detail below. The unit cost data base detailed item by item costs for materials (bags of cement, sand, nails, whitewash) and tasks (square yards of cobblestone laid, cubic meters of earth moved). The costs were differentiated by region, as necessary. The data base was built into an interactive system so that the project appraiser could input the number of units needed for a project and receive the recommended costs in detail and various standard aggregations. Adequate security measures were built in so that only authorized persons could change the unit prices themselves.

A third component of the information system was a separate data base on regional poverty characteristics used mainly by the promotion and appraisal departments to inform their targeting analysis.

The remarkable feature of the management information system was not so much the novelty of its design or software, but its use. Some aspect of it was used virtually every day by all of the professional staff, who manipulated it with ease.

The major flaw within the information system was that comprehensive though the summary indicators may have been, they did not contain information on the projects' quality aspects. For example, the rate of return was calculated during the appraisal of some types of projects, but this information was not entered into the data base. Rather it remained on paper in the individual project's file. Neither were indications of the quality of construction or impact on the beneficiaries codified. The information was acquired during project supervision, but not systematized. A second flaw was that the various sub-systems were essentially separate rather than integrated.

Donor Management. The ESF took an extremely flexible posture toward donors, and was willing to accept several different types of assistance. Donors contributed: (a) straight monetary resources; (b) convertible resources (e.g., Canada donated wheat, which the ESF then sold on international markets); and (c) non-convertible resources (e.g., Italy contributed materials for erosion control, which were put to use in ESF-financed projects).

As of April 30, 1990, donors had committed $197.1 million in monetary resources, $34.1 million in convertible resources and $8.3 million in non-convertible resources, for a total of $239.5 million. The list of donors includes multilateral agencies, foreign governments or their agencies, and one NGO. In particular:

Multilateral Agencies: Inter-American Development Bank, OPEC Fund for International Development, UNDP, World Bank.

Foreign Governments (or agencies thereof): Belgium, Canada, Federal Republic of Germany, Italy, Japan, Netherlands, Sweden, Switzerland, United Kingdom, United States.
NGO: Save the Children.

The nature of the accountability relationship that the ESF maintained with its donors is noteworthy as an interesting departure from the norm in externally financed development funds. The ESF did not permit donors to design their own projects; rather, donors were expected to endorse the ESF as a funding intermediary who would channel their contributions to worthy projects. At most, a donor could request that its funding go to a project (or projects) already approved by the ESF, or that its funding be directed to a particular sector — social infrastructure, for example. These donors could later ask the ESF to provide an after-the-fact accounting to show that their support had indeed been put toward the designated projects or sectors. However, the ESF would not, as a rule, entertain a request from a donor that its money be applied to a specific project at a specific location. From the ESF's point of view, this approach fit with the high priority it placed on having as much freedom as possible to act quickly and with flexibility. It avoided the problem faced by other development funds of being constrained in their operations by the varying demands and priorities of a diverse group of donors. Three major donors— Sweden, the Netherlands and Switzerland—committed their funding to be administered by the World Bank, under the same rules as World Bank funds.

The ESF's Project Cycle

The project cycle consisted of four phases (see Figure 1.2): promotion, appraisal, final approval and supervision.

Promotion. The aim of the promotion phase was to generate project proposals of high quality and of benefit to the poor that could then be passed on to the ESF's appraisal staff. The ESF, being a demand-driven institution, depended on the capacity of organizations throughout the country to conceive and prepare project proposals. But except for government agencies in urban areas, few organizations — particularly local or grassroots groups — had the experience or technical expertise to present a project in a way that would satisfy the scrutiny of the ESF. Moreover, many agencies in remote parts of the country simply had not heard of the ESF. Other groups, conditioned by years of inaction on the part of central government agencies, were skeptical that the ESF would keep its promises. Promotion department staff attacked these problems of inexperience, ignorance and skepticism by travelling widely throughout Bolivia, "marketing" the idea of the ESF. Numerous workshops were held, where promotion staff would assure local groups that the ESF meant business, was eager to receive project proposals, and could help groups that did not know how to prepare a formal project submission to get the necessary assistance. NGOs were a particular target of the promotion department, because of their reluctance to work with a government agency such as the

Figure 1.2 ESF Project Flow (as of April 30, 1990)

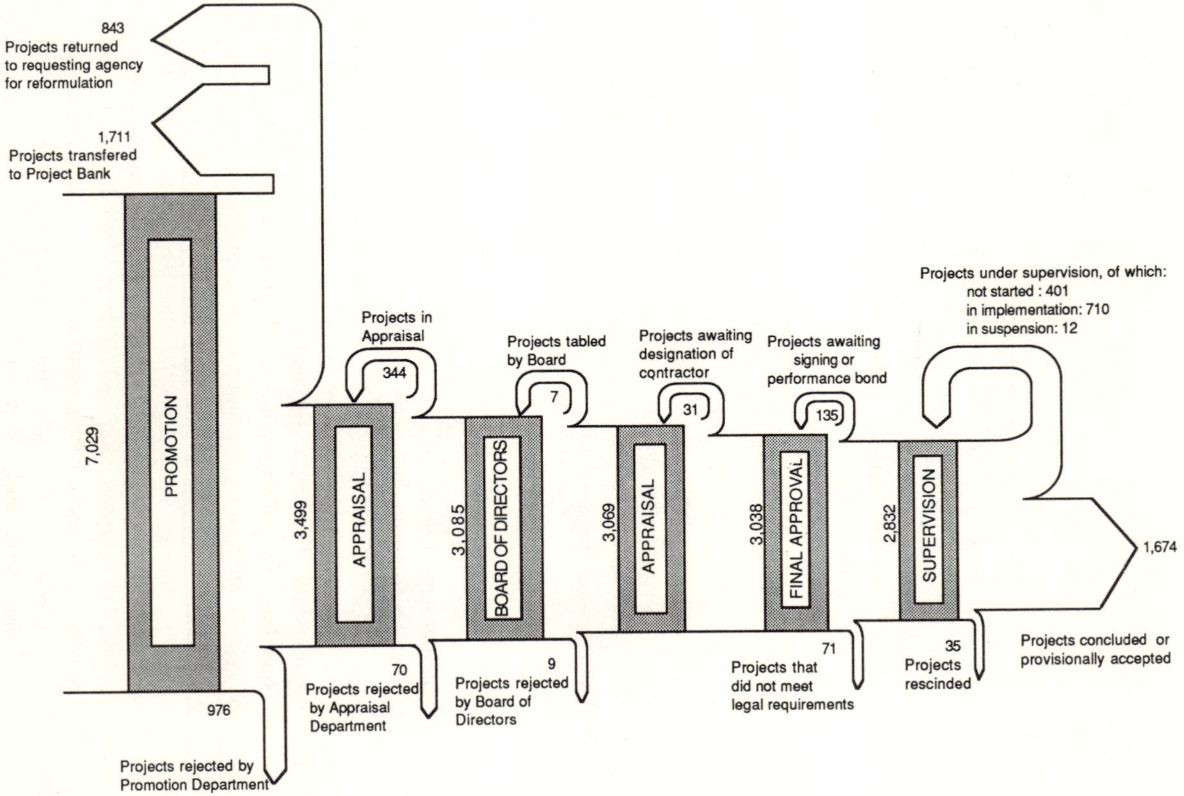

Source: ESF

ESF (see Chapter 6). Pains were taken to hire into the promotion staff persons who could relate particularly well to the concerns and priorities of NGOs.

The impact of the promotion team may be measured by the fact that while in 1987 only 10 percent of project proposals received by the ESF were deemed to be "appraisable", the ratio had climbed to 80 percent by the end of the following year.

Besides functioning to drum up interest in the ESF, the promotion unit also had a role to play as the first and most important screen in the project cycle. Of the 7,000 projects that had been seen by the promotion department as of April 30, 1990, only 3,500 had been passed on to the next stage of the cycle. In some cases, projects would be rejected outright if they were poorly formulated, or if they clearly did not meet the ESF's broad criterion of serving the poor. In other cases, project proposals that were both properly formulated and well suited to benefiting the poor may have been turned back because the communities they were intended to serve were in a region of Bolivia from which the ESF already had a surfeit of project submissions. Rather than being rejected outright, these proposals, which were essentially sound, were placed in the ESF's "project bank" for possible reconsideration at a later date. (Ultimately many of these were passed to the ESF's successor organization, the Social Investment Fund.)

Appraisal. Once through promotion, projects entered appraisal. Midway through its second year of operation, the ESF's appraisal department had produced a 160-page "Appraisal Guide," which was a distillation of its experience to date, and which became the basis for the comprehensive system of project appraisal used by the ESF. The essential feature of the Guide was that it standardized, to the greatest degree possible, the task of the appraisal staff, thereby enabling them to work quickly while also ensuring that they would consistently apply similar appraisal criteria across a broad range of projects.

The Guide took the four basic types of projects funded by the ESF and broke them down into 12 sub-types.[3] For each sub-type, the Guide set out the ESF's estimates of the unit costs, magnitude and composition of key elements of a hypothetical, "typical" project. The Guide provided the staff member (called the appraiser) with data on the overall size and total cost of the typical project, the origin and type of labor and materials required (skilled vs. non-skilled, local vs. imported), the cost to the ESF for each person-month of employment created by the project, and the unit price to be paid to the project contractor for each material component of the project (e.g. a square meter of tiled flooring would be worth a standard amount, as would a linear meter of electrical wiring). The appraiser compared the typical quantities and prices with those contained in the actual project proposal: if any of the figures in the actual project proposal were to differ substantially from the standard amounts in the Guide, the appraiser might decide to send the proposal back to the sponsor for reformulation. If, by contrast, the appraiser were to approve a project containing non-standard elements, he would have to explain formally his decision when recommending the project for approval. The appraiser might decide, for example, that the unit prices in the Guide did not adequately reflect local conditions, and therefore would have to be adjusted.

The unit cost system was developed to ensure reasonable costs under the nontraditional procurement system. Initially, the costs were determined by informal market surveys for items available at retail markets and by adding transportation costs to bulk goods prices for items such as cement and roofing sheets. Salaries were determined by adding a cost factor to the prevailing levels in La Paz, and productivity determined by "educated guesses." Later on all prices were checked regularly, and twice annually full audits were performed to ensure the validity of the unit costs.

The Guide also contained a series of checklists for the appraiser, enumerating steps he should be sure to take both before making a visit to the site of the proposed project and during the site visit. To see how this would work in practice, following are examples of how an ESF appraiser would draw upon the Guide when appraising a social infrastructure project (building a school) and an economic infrastructure project (upgrading work on a highway).

Building a School. The first point the appraiser encountered in the Guide was a list of essential documents to be submitted by the project sponsor:

- correctly completed project proposal forms;
- architectural plans;
- plans for any type of equipment or hardware to be installed;
- detailed construction plans;
- technical specifications; and
- project memorandum including details on the expected beneficiary population and their needs.

The Guide then described a typical rural school construction project. The typical school house should have false ceilings, cement floors and adobe walls (with a thickness of 20 centimeters), surfaced on the outside with lime-cement and on the interior with plaster. It should cover 57 square meters, and have a unit construction cost of $80.25 per square meter, making for a total cost of $4574.25. The unit cost to the ESF for each person-month of employment generated by the project is $375.

A full accounting was given of all the activities necessary to complete the typical project, with unit costs and total costs for each. The budget shows, for example, that the building should require 66.8 square meters of exterior paint, at a unit price of $1.81, for a total cost of $120.91. Project costs are broken down both by activity and by type of labor and materials. The activity breakdown is given as a unit cost for each square meter of school:

Preliminary Work	$0.27
Foundations	4.85
Walls	4.38
Roofing	23.34
Plastering and Painting	27.21
Flooring	12.49
Carpentry	7.71
Total Unit Cost	$80.25

Materials and labor are broken down in terms of percentage of total project cost:

Domestic Material	53 percent
Imported Material	3 percent
Skilled Labor	20 percent
Unskilled Labor	10 percent
Imported Tools and Equipment	1 percent
Administration	13 percent
Total	100 percent

Following the section on unit costs was a checklist of items or issues the appraiser should be sure to examine closely before making a site visit. They included:

- architectural plans and technical specifications;
- the availability of electrical and sanitary services;
- the amount of labor required by the proposed project;
- the cost per square meter of construction implied by the proposal;
- land title;
- the existing state of local educational services; and
- the continuing availability of administrative resources, services and equipment once the school has been built.

Another checklist enumerated key points for the appraiser to note during the site visit:

- population of the area to be served by the school;
- number of students the school was likely to serve;
- other existing educational services in the area;
- location of the land to be used for the project;
- local availability of construction material;
- local availability of labor;
- local institutional capacity for execution and supervision of the project;
- local prices for labor, materials and transportation; and
- knowledge of the project on the part of intended beneficiaries.

Because this was an education construction project, the appraiser was not required to do a cost-benefit analysis. The reasoning stated in the Guide was that "benefits in education are difficult to quantify due to a lack of statistical data" in Bolivia. In lieu of a cost-benefit analysis, the appraiser was required to calculate the cost of the project per beneficiary.

Having completed the appraisal and decided that the proposal was suitable for presentation to the ESF's board of directors for final approval, the appraiser summarized these findings by filling out a standard appraisal form for education projects that was sent to the board.

Upgrading a Road. The format followed by the Guide was much the same here as for the school project, with the same types of checklists, a description of the size and unit cost of the "typical" project (26 kilometers of road at $5,101 per kilometer), and a cost breakdown by activity and by type of labor and materials. The principal difference was that in this case, the appraiser was required to do a cost-benefit analysis of the project.

The ESF developed a simple, standard formula for cost-benefit analyses of road maintenance projects. An assumption was made that any road, if maintained, would last for ten years, while the same road, unmaintained, would have a life of only five years. Using straight line depreciation, and a discount rate of 12 percent, the present value of the stream of costs (i.e., the annual depreciation) of the maintained road was compared to that of the unmaintained road. If the net present value of the costs for the maintained road was lower, the project would be approved. The following table provides an example:

	Upgraded Road	*Existing Road*
Current Value of Road	$100,000	$100,000
Cost of Upgrading	10,000	0
Total Value of Road	110,000	100,000
Life of Road	10 years	5 years
Annual Depreciation	11,000	20,000
Discount Rate	12 %	12 %
NPV of Depreciation	$62,152	$72,096

Because the net present value of the future cost stream of the upgraded road was lower than that for the unimproved road, the decision would be to approve the project.

Final Approval. Having been approved by an appraiser and given final approval by the board of directors, the project was passed to the ESF's legal department for the drafting of a contract. The contract, among other things, made a take-it-or-leave-it offer to the project contractor (see below) to undertake the work for the price determined by the ESF appraiser based on the unit cost system. Generally speaking, contracts for ESF works were not procured by open bidding. (For details on the ESF's unit cost method of procurement, see Chapter 5.)

Each contract drafted for an ESF project was a four-part agreement involving:

- the ESF as *financier*;
- the group that proposed the project as *sponsor*; for example, a sponsoring agency might be an NGO seeking funding for a child nutrition project, a municipality requesting funds for street paving or the education ministry seeking funds to build or repair a school;
- a *supervising agency*, whose role was to monitor the quality of the implementation of the project; the supervisor would be recommended by the sponsor and approved by the ESF; the ESF would want to ensure that the supervisor had adequate technical qualifications; for example, an engineer

would be an appropriate supervisor for a construction or street-paving project while a nutritionist would be appropriate for a nutrition project; and

- a *contractor*, nominated by the sponsor, who had the job of implementing the project; a construction company would be the contractor for a school-building project, while an NGO might be the contractor for a nutrition project.

Although there were always four parties to the contract, there were not always four different entities involved. In some cases, the sponsor and the supervisor might be the same agency. (A municipality might sponsor a sewerage project, and use its own engineers to supervise it.) In other cases, the sponsor might also be the contractor. (This was particularly common with social assistance projects, which were often sponsored and delivered by NGOs.) Some configurations never occurred: the ESF would not permit the contractor and supervisor to be the same party; the ESF, of course, acted always and only as financier.

Supervision. With the contract signed, the project entered the supervision phase, where procedures governing the disbursement of funds to the contractor came into effect. To enable the contractor to begin working, the ESF advanced an amount equal to 20 percent of the project's budget. At the same time, as security against this advance, the ESF required the contractor to secure a bank's guarantee of repayment of the 20 percent advance in the event that the contractor failed to perform on the contract. (It was not always a simple matter for contractors to raise the performance bond. In some cases, the contractor asked the project's sponsor to raise the bond.)

The rest of the project's budget was disbursed to the contractor gradually, as stages of the work were completed. In infrastructure projects, the supervisor and the ESF zone chief would visit the project site about once a month to observe the quality and quantity of progress. If 10 percent of the work was completed satisfactorily between site visits, the zone chief would advise the ESF to advance a further 10 percent of the budget (minus a proportional amount of the original 20 percent advance) to the contractor. Where social assistance projects were concerned, the site visits focused on ensuring that the services envisioned by the project were actually being delivered. For a nutrition program, the following might be checked: How many meals have been served? Was the food of acceptable quality? Was the food of the right type?

Once disbursements were approved, they were paid quickly, a measure that gained the confidence and goodwill of contractors. The disbursement schedule was timed so that the last portion of funding was not paid to the contractor until all work was complete. The ESF aimed for a turnaround time between approval and payment of about two weeks. (For more detail on sub-project implementation, particularly the ESF's experience with cost-overruns, sub-project delays, sub-project supervisors, and the technical quality of the works funded by the ESF, see Chapter 3.)

Visual Impact

The impacts of the ESF can be seen in the following case studies. These examples show projects which illustrate the directive to provide services and infrastructure to poor communities.

El Alto

El Alto, sprawled out on a barren 13,000 foot high plain above the Bolivian capital, La Paz, is a child of the country's economic misfortune in the 1980s. Over the past ten years, its population has swelled from 100,000 to 350,000 as peasants from the countryside, laid off miners from towns around Oruro and Potosi, and other victims of the economic crisis emigrated to La Paz in search of work. El Alto's houses are built of adobe bricks, many of its streets are unpaved and potholed, less than half its inhabitants have running water in their homes, and only about one in five houses is connected to a sewerage system. A microcosm of Bolivian poverty, El Alto was a primary target for the ESF, which committed about $12 million to projects there.

Now, the town is criss-crossed by excavations for sewerage works funded by the ESF. The need for them is plain: in neighborhoods that are not hooked up to sewers, small waste pipes from each house empty directly on to the street. In some areas, whole sections of road lie under ankle-deep pools of stagnant brown water.

On a wintry, windy, late afternoon, a group of boys is playing soccer on the grounds of Colegio Zona Santiago Primero, a high school constructed with $100,000 from the ESF. One of the soccer players is Nemecio Marca, president of the students council. "The other schools around here were either overcrowded or a long walk away. We'd rather go to this one," he said, though he added that he would be happier if the school had a library.

Not far from the school, mothers are coming into the Centro Infantil Integral to fetch their children at the end of the day. The daycare center, which opened in September 1988, was built with $43,000 from the ESF. The center, staffed by five teachers, has classes for the children, and meals: breakfast, a mid-morning snack, lunch, and an afternoon snack. Parents are charged a small fee.

"These mothers have to work to help support the family. Some can hardly afford to feed their children properly," said Daisy Rodriquez, one of the teachers.

In another neighborhood, Juana Canqui is standing with her four children in the doorway of her small house. The family used to live in a small town southeast of La Paz, where her husband was a miner. They migrated to El Alto after he lost his job in the cutbacks at the state-owned mining company.

"We came to El Alto in 1986, and at first we lived in a plastic tent," she said.

Today she and her husband own their house, one of 105 homes in a low-cost housing project funded by the ESF. Each of the small two-bedroom houses cost $2,000 to construct, but the purchase price is set at about $1,400, which the owners pay back at low interest over 20 years.

Guayamerin

In the northeast corner of Bolivia, in the jungle lowlands of the Amazon basin, Guayamerin sits on the banks of the broad, brown Rio Mamore. The Brazilian city of Guajara Mirim is a short boat ride away on the opposite shore.

The Mamore sometimes overflows its banks during the rainy season, dislodging the farmers who set up stalls on a strip of land near the river's edge where they sell the bananas, grapefruit, lemons and oranges that they bring down the river by boat. "When it floods, we have to pack everything up and move it over there," said Ramon Noco, pointing to a nearby street. The ESF granted the town $26,000 to build a covered farmers' market on a raised concrete platform.

"I am definitely going to use the new market. It will be much more comfortable, and cleaner," said Lenni Gonzales who brings bananas into town from a farm about a mile upriver.

The rainy season causes problems for residents, too. A stream that passes through a residential area floods during the rains, damaging property and washing out streets. "Around here, the road turns into a lake," said the mayor, Guido Rocco, pointing to a spot where the streambed passes under the street. In a channel across the street where the stream reappears, about a dozen men stand calf-deep, barefoot in the water, digging with small shovels, and throwing the clayey mush up onto the banks. The work is part of a $215,000 flood control channel funded by the ESF.

Just next to where the men are working stands a building that until very recently was used as an elementary school. It is little better than a lean-to, made of rickety timbers with big spaces in between, and completely open to the weather on one side. There is no floor, no blackboard. A grant of $350,000 from the ESF has funded the construction of five modern elementary schools, and a further $62,000 paid for the manufacture of 2,000 desks.

Domitila de Guardia, a teacher at the Fedex Chaco school, which opened in February 1989, said the new building is a stark contrast to where she used to work. "There were so many holes in the roof it rained more inside than out," she said.

A remote city in a sparsely populated region far from the center of power in Bolivia, Guayamerin was unaccustomed to benefitting from government largesse. When the school construction projects were first announced, "no one here believed that they would actually happen," Rocco said.

Santa Cruz

The suburb of Villa Primero de Mayo lies in the southeast outskirts of Santa Cruz, Bolivia's second-largest city. It is a poor neighborhood, inhabited by street vendors, unskilled laborers, washerwomen, single-parent mothers, and young people who have flocked here to find work. Ten years ago perhaps 4,000 people lived in Villa Primero de Mayo; today there are 70,000. Its growth has mirrored that of Santa Cruz itself, which was home to about 40,000 people 40 years ago, and is home to about 700,000 today. Major discoveries of natural gas and increasing agricultural development in the region, as well as the burgeoning cocaine trade, have drawn migrants to the city. The Health Center/"Micro Hospital" Primero de Mayo is run privately by a Catholic church organization. It has a full-time staff of three doctors who see about 70 patients a day, at a fee of five bolivianos (about $1.75) per visit. Malnutrition, dehydration, respiratory problems and anemia are among the most commonly seen ailments; much of the ill health in the district can be traced to the fact that it has no sanitary sewerage system. In a neighborhood populated mainly by young men, women, and children, it is the young women and children who use the hospital most, so time is set aside each day for clinics in gynecology, pediatrics and obstetrics. There is also instruction for women in hygiene and child nutrition.

Funding from the ESF is paying for construction of an X-ray room, kitchen, storage room, cafeteria and common room, and an overnight room for the doctor who is on call.

"We heard about some projects that the ESF had funded, and we thought we would give it a try. There was nothing to lose," one of the doctors said. "We hadn't seen any help from the government over the past ten years. Any improvements we have received, like water or electricity, have been through our own efforts."

Near the hospital is the Villa Primero de Mayo Cultural Center, one of nine cultural centers built in and around Santa Cruz with $320,000 from the ESF. The center offers courses and seminars in areas such as artistic design, clothes-making, and the administration of cultural centers. It also sponsors folklore festivals.

"In recent years people have come from all over Bolivia to live in Santa Cruz. This creates huge problems in terms of adaptation and integration. That's what we're trying to do with the cultural centers; help integrate people into society," said Marcelo Arauz, director of Culture House, the organization that runs the cultural centers.

Perhaps the most important service provided by Culture House is its small network of libraries, one of which is at the Villa Primero de Mayo Cultural Center. Neighborhood high school students depend on its 1,500 book collection for help with their homework because Santa Cruz, though one of Bolivia's major cities, has no system of public libraries.

"The local authorities have many things to do, and culture is not a priority for them," Arauz said.

Concluding Note

The foregoing outline of the origins of the ESF, its structure and procedures, and its accomplishments sets the necessary contextual backdrop for the material that follows. Some of the subsequent chapters expand on issues that have already been identified here, such as the unique nature of the ESF's procurement procedures, the pragmatic design of the ESF's targeting mechanism, and the importance of the links created between the ESF and NGOs. Other chapters take up new themes, such as the impact of the ESF on workers at the projects it funded, and the economics of a demand-driven investment fund.

As has been noted, the ESF was from its inception intended to be a temporary institution, and its termination was scheduled for the end of March 1991. Much of its work was taken over by traditional state agencies, but a part of its portfolio—health and education projects—was handed over to a newly created, permanent government agency, the Social Investment Fund, which will receive funding from the World Bank and other external donors.

Notes

1. All dollar amounts are U.S. dollars.

2. Data on the actual impact of government subsidies on various income groups in Bolivia were not available.

3. The *social assistance* category was subdivided into food and nutrition, health, training and educational assistance; *social infrastructure* was subdivided into potable water and sanitation, housing, construction in the health sector (e.g. health posts), construction in the education sector, and cultural projects (e.g. restoration of monuments); and *economic infrastructure* was subdivided into urban improvement, access roads, drainage and irrigation, and erosion control and reforestation. The *production support* category was not subdivided.

2

The Genesis and Early Debates

by Katherine Marshall

This chapter relates the tale of the Emergency Social Fund's establishment, from the perspective of the World Bank, with a focus on some key turning points and on how some perennially thorny issues were tackled.

Genesis

Bolivia's New Economic Policy (NEP), as the Paz Estenssoro government's economic stabilization and adjustment program was known, was launched virtually full-blown about three weeks after the government took office in August 1985. The small group of Bolivian officials and their advisors who designed the program were aware of the plight of Bolivia's people, but did not focus explicitly on what has since come to be termed the "social dimensions of adjustment." Awareness of political interests was clear, but the conviction was so firm that the proposed economic reforms constituted the only possible salvation for the nation as a whole, that measures to cushion the impact of adjustment on specific social groups were not at the forefront of the discussion. In the first year of the NEP, explicit social policy issues took a low priority, except in specific response to crises (for example, the prolonged teachers' strike).

This changed in the fall of 1986, as the government came to view action to address social issues as critical to the success of the NEP and, indeed, to its own survival. The precipitating cause was a crescendo of protests, most strikingly a march of miners and their families on La Paz in response to massive layoffs at COMIBOL, the state-owned mining company. Intensive debate ensued on what action should be taken, with heavy emphasis on the urgent need for visible and effective measures to help those immediately affected by the adjustment policies, in the first instance the miners. The president and his senior ministers began to push for a rapid response and for immediate international assistance. The United Nations took a strong and visible position advocating action and support. There was strong verbal and political support for the government's initiative from several donors. Tangible aid was forthcoming only in small amounts, however, because the concept of social action was still very general, and mechanisms for channeling assistance only vaguely defined.

Indeed, over roughly the next two years Bolivia faced a dichotomy in the position taken by potential external donors: on the one hand a strong and swelling sympathy, inspired by the struggle of the government and the magnitude of the obstacles it faced; on the other, a deep-seated cynicism about Bolivia's capacity and will to make fundamental changes, born of decades of economic mismanagement, disappointing use of external assistance, and widespread corruption. Although there was extensive verbal and moral support of Bolivia's program, this was coupled with a reluctance to commit funds in the absence of solid guarantees of honest and effective administration and staying power in carrying through the program.

The World Bank took a central part in the Bolivian debate on social issues during the fall of 1986. The Bank had been an early supporter of the government's economic program: indeed, the Bank's analyses had served as an important source of ideas for the Bolivian economic team. During 1985-86 the Bank moved ahead quickly with a renewed program of assistance, launched with a $55 million credit. Despite a strong awareness of social issues, however, the early program did not focus on them. From September 1986, Bank staff were involved in intensive discussions with the economic team about the Consultative Group (CG) meeting that took place in December 1986.[1] This proved to be the mechanism through which social issues moved to the top of the agenda for both the Bank and the government as they prepared to present the economic program and priorities for external assistance to a highly visible forum of international financiers.

At the same time that the social policy agenda came to occupy a central place in the broad discussions of economic policy, the chance presence in Bolivia of a Bank consultant (on private sector development) who was a politician (a British Member of Parliament) helped to crystallize the issues and the debate. He helped to convince the Bank staff that the need for highly visible action to address social issues was crucial and immediate. Measures comprising a blend of hard-nosed technical and economic analysis, a longer term vision of social policy directions, and the recognition that all the adjustment measures and outstanding economic management would be useless if political forces swamped and overturned the government were required. The Bolivian economic team, meanwhile, had become absolutely convinced that a prompt, substantial, effective and visible social action program was of paramount importance.

Intensive work was launched to design a social action program, led by a well respected and dynamic Bolivian business man, Fernando Romero. Romero took some pride in asserting that he had never served in government, though he had been an *eminence gris* in the design and execution of the NEP. Appointed as executive director of the ESF in November 1986, he immediately began to design from scratch an agency that would combine the attributes of an effective private company with a strong sense of social purpose.

When the government came to the CG in Paris in early December 1986, the ESF had been formally established by a decree signed the night the Bolivian delegation left La Paz for Paris. The Bolivians made an urgent plea to the World Bank to take a central role in helping to launch the new ESF, and to the international community for immediate and substantial financial support. The ESF as presented to the CG was still embryonic, but it included many of the central features that guaranteed its later success, and that attracted the support of the international community.

Since Romero wanted to begin operations in three months, the proposal represented a challenge thrown to the donor agencies gathered, many of which were accustomed to taking two years to approve projects for financing. Initial response at the Paris meeting was very positive "in principle," but was predictably cautious in dollar terms. The Bank delegation, with some consternation given the controversial nature of the program, agreed to assist in the detailed design of the ESF and to help mobilize international financing, but made no promises on level of support or timing of its receipt.

The months following the CG were somewhat frustrating for the Bolivian team, and especially for Romero, who proceeded to set up an organization and prepare for action. He confidently expected to see external support flow within three months. The Bank was involved during this period (early 1987), pursuing the debates on design, objectives, and means that had started in the fall of 1986. These exchanges were part of a genuine partnership that had emerged and was to persist throughout the life of the ESF, and helped to shape its operating procedures and philosophy. However, although the essential groundwork of support was being established, Bank money was not instantly available.

During the early spring of 1987, Romero visited Washington and met with senior Bank officials. His down-to-earth, pragmatic approach did much to dispel the skepticism that greeted his proposal to move very swiftly with what appeared to be a vast, under-designed public works scheme that had unhealthy shades of relief activities in which the Bank's charter prohibited involvement. Also vital in the effort to gather support was the increasing attention being paid at the Bank and other institutions to the issue of "social costs of adjustment," dramatized by a major UNICEF report urging "adjustment with a human face." Within the Bank, a special Task Force on Poverty took a positive interest in the embryonic Bolivian scheme, and discussions were launched with NGOs and academics to enlist ideas, criticism, and support. The Swiss government, approached to be an early partner in what was admittedly a risky venture, agreed, and the way was paved.

Work within the Bank to process the credit to support the ESF was begun in early 1987. The work was disrupted by an internal reorganization effort that took place at the Bank between April and July 1987, but the credit moved forward with a speed almost unknown in an institution renowned (often unfairly) for its slow, deliberate pace of operation. A credit for $10 million was approved in June 1987.

The Board of Executive Directors gave an unusually enthusiastic response. There was clearly a strong groundswell of support for a program designed to provide direct support for the poor affected by economic crisis and adjustment measures.

The interest of the Bank in the ESF was attested to by the speed with which the first credit was approved. That the Bank had some reservations about the ESF was manifested in unusual provisions for oversight and review. The Bank reserved the right to review *every* project prior to approving disbursement for it. Even under the second Bank credit for the ESF, the Bank reviewed all projects costing more than $50,000, and a generous sample of those under that amount. This close supervision was unusual and demanded far more staff time than the norm. In addition, more project impact evaluation than usual was programmed (see Chapter 3), and regular reviews of procurement were required (see Chapter 5).

For all its rapidity, the Bank's assistance came none too soon, for the ESF had already begun operations. Projects presented by communities and NGOs were being screened and approved for financing with advance funding provided by the Bolivian government. Staff had been hired and were promoting the scheme on the ground and through the media throughout Bolivia. The ESF and the Bank jointly launched concentrated efforts to mobilize external financing, which proved highly successful.

The Debates

The early debates that occurred during the formative period of the ESF determined its basic design and helped account for much of its success, both in operational terms and in garnering support within Bolivia and among the international donor community. To be sure, current understanding of the social aspects of adjustment is far more sophisticated than it was in late 1986, as are notions of targeting assistance, and techniques of analyzing the priority of social needs. However, the essential question of how to design an effective program, steering between the theoretical ideals of achieving social justice and the realities of operating as part of a complex adjustment program with intensive political and social pressures, was squarely addressed in the Bolivian case.

A vital factor in those early discussions was the partnership that emerged between Bank staff and government officials: this was an environment where the goals and basic diagnosis were shared and where there was strong mutual confidence in the qualities and motivations of the parties concerned.

Poverty: The Result of the Adjustment or the Precipitating Crisis?

The debate in the fall of 1986 started with the nature of the problem to be addressed: what kind of poverty was at issue, and how far should it be linked to the adjustment measures the government had launched in 1985? The Bolivian government, then and subsequently, was reluctant to agree that social problems resulted from its policies, and it made the valid argument that most of Bolivia's social ills were the result of the decades of economic mismanagement and especially of the economic crisis of the early 1980s. It argued forcefully that without the adjustment measures the economy would have collapsed, and the poor would have become even more destitute. Indeed, social spending had increased since the implementation of the NEP, and there was already at least a semblance of more normal operation of key public services. Improvements in food supply were also in evidence as elaborate regulations were dismantled and distorting price controls were removed.

Yet clearly there were numerous ways in which adjustment measures (for example, the elimination of food and input price subsidies and the reduction in employment in some government entities) had to have a direct impact on people, often (but by no means always) in the lower income groups. Perhaps equally important, there was a widespread perception, inside and outside Bolivia, that the adjustment measures were having a cruel impact on the population. The dismal state of data on social conditions in Bolivia aggravated the problem and stultified intelligent debate; social statistics had long been poor, and the hyperinflationary years had rendered virtually all income figures meaningless. Most evidence was anecdotal and sharply contrasting versions of reality were presented.

On this issue—was the problem economic crisis or structural adjustment?—the solution was to beg the question and to focus on the social problems themselves, not on what or who had caused them and when. The objective, agreed then and reiterated since, was to address the major social problems that had resulted from the years of economic crisis and from the effects of adjustment measures.

The Poorest of the Poor? The New Poor?

The next major issue was how much poverty to address, and where to draw the line. This demanded some hard choices, given the magnitude of poverty in Bolivia. Administratively, technically, and financially, no emergency program could address even a small fraction of the problem. Further, a large part of the poorest lived in quite remote rural areas. They were neither those most affected by the crisis or adjustment, nor were they reachable on a substantial scale by an emergency program, no matter how well designed or run. The difficult circumstances of Bolivia, the absence of data, the lack of clarity about how to develop agriculture, and so on, precluded focusing solely on the poorest. The principle was established that targeting would be handled in a broad framework, by major economic sector and region, rather than by attempting to direct the programs to affected individuals.

The Focus on Miners

A continual tension in the program was to define the extent to which the miners, who were the most politically active and visible group, and who clearly suffered from losing their jobs and from the death of many mining communities, were to be the principal targets of the ESF. COMIBOL was the highest cost tin producer in the world, and as the fulcrum of a powerful union movement, a central fixture in Bolivian politics. The NEP included much-needed measures to reduce COMIBOL's work force from some 30,000 to about 7,000. The shapers of the NEP were anxious to provide severance payments to the miners to muffle their reaction. (Such payments were also required by law.) The donor community (including the Bank, which had a long-standing involvement with efforts to rescue COMIBOL) and the international press tended to focus on the miners as the primary victims of adjustment measures. On the other hand, it was clear from the start that, with large legislated lay-off payments of up to $3000 per worker, the miners were in fact quite a privileged group. Here too, a pragmatic approach was adopted; miners were the subject of some special attention and efforts. For example, many were employed to construct mudslide-prevention works on the cliffs around La Paz, an undertaking that used tunneling techniques that suited the miners ideally. Even so, the miners were by no means the sole or central focus of the ESF program.

The Long Run Plan

The long term objective of the ESF was another subject of intensive reflection and debate. At first, the Bolivians found the topic theoretical and unrealistic. In the crisis that prevailed, the "long term" was next week, and it seemed futile to discuss a time horizon of ten years when the government's survival in 1987 was at issue. The Bank staff, on the other hand, was particularly insistent that the ESF be set in a medium- to long-term framework, leading to both national poverty alleviation efforts and a coherent administrative approach to handling basic social services. Without the longer term framework, the staff was convinced that the ESF could not garner the support of the Bank's senior management, Board, or other donors. Moreover, discussions with officials and academic leaders in the field also highlighted the potential problems of indefinite, long-lasting programs of employment or social assistance which were not integrated into the fabric of government. These included distortion of basic government and private sector programs, emergence of bloated bureaucracies, increasing temptation to corruption, and much greater political pressures shaping the programs as time went by.

Out of these opposed points of view there emerged a clear consensus that it was vital to set the ESF in a defined, temporary time frame: it could not be seen as the central answer to Bolivia's social and poverty issues, which required and demanded a much broader long term approach. Hence, the decision to limit the ESF to a three year life (the term was later extended by 15 months).

Social Assistance vs. Employment

One well-articulated school of thought maintained that the primary purpose of the ESF should be to provide targeted social assistance, along the lines of vaccination programs, school feeding, health centers, and day care programs. The practical obstacles to launching such a program quickly and on a large scale, given the institutional weaknesses in Bolivia and lack of data on what really needed to be and could be done, argued against this concept. The ultimately agreed upon target of 25 percent of ESF funds for such efforts reflected a judgement of how much could realistically be accomplished in the social assistance sphere.[2]

Selection Criteria

The initial impetus was to fund public works schemes, even ones implemented directly by the government, on the grounds that this would generate employment and could use immediately the labor of displaced miners. Ideas included road rehabilitation and school construction. However, after considerable debate within Bolivia, the idea of smaller projects, generated by communities themselves, largely in areas affected by the economic decline, won out. At the Bank's insistence, tight criteria for economic viability were agreed upon, and the ideas, pushed at the outset, of "painting monuments" and essentially accepting any scheme that involved high employment were quashed. The conviction grew that there were ample opportunities in Bolivia for productive investment that would meet economic rate of return criteria, and this proved to be the case.

Institutional Arrangements

Considerable discussion revolved around how the ESF was to be run. Two major questions had to be addressed: the basic locus of power and links to other Bolivian agencies, and the essential style of organization and management. The final decision to place the ESF directly under the presidency, with few formal links to existing agencies, was not only inherently controversial, but also called for an agency to be built from scratch, a somewhat unnerving prospect given the weakness of institutions in Bolivia. Contenders within the established bureaucracy for the potentially powerful and lucrative ESF were keen to have it integrated with their existing programs and were loath to contemplate the development of a new, potential rival. That they lost out in the end reflected the President's personal interest in and support for the program. Paz Estenssoro was well aware that only by elevating the ESF above the political fray and the bureaucracy could it operate efficiently.

On organization and style, the watchword from the outset was "private sector." The idea was to model the ESF on a dynamic, entrepreneurial outfit, bound by as few rules as possible, and driven by clearly defined goals and operating procedures. The tone was set by the provision in the ESF's charter that limited the proportion of total funds that it could spend on administration. The ESF's independent status made dynamism and efficiency possible. As it emerged, it bore little resemblance to the caricature of a Bolivian public entity: sleepy, overstaffed, underpaid, and lethargic in operation. The ESF employed young people, primarily with private sector experience, introduced computerized systems, and prided itself on its reporting techniques and speed of action. The staff was well paid by Bolivian standards, and was deeply committed to the mission of the institution. In Bolivia's exceptionally difficult environment, the ESF model gave hope and showed what could be done, even if the Bolivians themselves and their external supporters were inclined to despair that the government's ambitious goals could ever be achieved.

On the nuts and bolts of management, the pragmatic and experienced approach of the executive director and the mutual confidence between the ESF and external financiers made it possible to resolve almost instantly debates that have sunk similar efforts elsewhere. For example, there was instant agreement on external audit procedures and publication of financial statements, designed to make clear that financial management would be transparent and absolutely honest. Impact monitoring proposals, though they initially seemed somewhat academic to the Bolivian staff, were accepted, and the Bolivians came to see that there were tangible benefits to be derived from mechanisms to evaluate the impact of programs from the outset.

Conclusion

The genesis of the ESF was, in sum, an effective joint venture between a government under intense pressure to pursue an adjustment program and to find effective ways to translate into action its principles of wishing to help the poor, and a donor community that was groping toward ways to translate its laudable but ill-defined principles into practical support. The story is heartening because of the happy outcome, and for this the Bolivian government's and the ESF's leadership and vision were almost entirely responsible. But credit is also due to Bolivia's external partners, who involved themselves deeply in the effort to shape a worthwhile program that they could support, and that would lead toward the long range goal of promoting social development for Bolivia and for its poor population. The dialectic that emerged led, through both debate and action, to a constructive blend of external experience, healthy skepticism, vision and hope, pragmatism and compromise. A basic message of Bolivia's ESF experience is that the seemingly impossible, though difficult, can sometimes be achieved.

Notes

1. The Consultative Group is comprised of the bilateral and multilateral agencies which provide external financing to aid in Bolivia's development.
2. In the other chapters of this book, the goal is given as 10 percent. In fact, in the earliest conception, the goal was 25 percent for social programs, the definition of which was somewhat unclear. In a later reprogramming and redefinition, social infrastructure and social assistance projects were put into separate categories, with targets of 45 and 10 percent, respectively.

3

How Well Did the ESF Work? A Review of Its Evaluations

by Margaret Grosh

This chapter surveys the substantial body of evaluations that have been conducted on the Bolivian Emergency Social Fund (ESF), with a view to assessing how well it worked. The individual evaluation studies that the chapter reviews are listed in Box 3.1, with brief descriptions of their methods. The administrative accomplishments of the ESF are described in terms of costs, project delays and suspensions, and technical quality. The bulk of the chapter reviews the impact of ESF activities in various ways. The last section draws out some of the lessons of these evaluations for similar organizations being established elsewhere.

Two of the lessons should perhaps be mentioned in advance—even with the plethora of evaluations, many of the important questions about the ESF's impact remain only partly answered. There are several reasons for this. The ESF's goal and standards evolved over its life, so that the original focus on evaluating the impact on worker's income was broadened and other studies were introduced. Several of these were commissioned on an *ad hoc* basis with little in the way of systematic design or data collection. The studies, therefore, made what they could of available data, which were frequently insufficient to produce definitive answers. Additionally, some of the studies suffered from vague terms of reference, inadequate supervision or poor technical work. A more comprehensive, preplanned monitoring and evaluation plan at the beginning of the ESF might have produced more satisfactory answers to the question—How well did the ESF work? With these general warnings in mind, this chapter extracts the conclusions from the somewhat uneven literature reviewed.

A second lesson is that in evaluating the ESF it is important to specify whether it is being measured against an ideal standard or against other development projects (in Bolivia or around the world). The latter is clearly more useful, but

Box 3.1 A Plethora of Evaluations

Administrative Statistics

ESF Data Base. The ESF maintained an excellent information system which tracked each project from the proposal stage through to completion. Information on project location, size, person-months of labor required, cost, number of beneficiaries, state of advancement, etc. was available. Detailed cash flow and commitment profiles of the ESF's portfolio were regularly produced. Records were kept of contracting arrangements, the construction delays, cost adjustments, etc.

Technical Audit. In 1988 the ESF commissioned an independent evaluation of the technical/engineering quality of its civil works. The results were used to correct implementation problems in individual projects. New analysis of the data base was performed here to look at correlates of project quality.

Formal Evaluations

Evaluation and Monitoring Report. The ESF contracted an outside team of economists and sociologists for a review of ESF activities and their impact after the first year of operations (Castaños, *et al.*, 1988).

Community Participation. The ESF contracted a team of anthropologists for a participant observation study (Molino Rivera, *et al.*, 1988). The study evaluated the reactions of ESF workers, contractors, community leaders and community members through open-ended, but structured interviews.

Workers' Incomes. The World Bank undertook an econometric evaluation of the ESF's benefits in terms of employment and wages for its workers (Newman, Jorgensen, Pradhan, 1991, see also Chapter 4). Collection of the data was financed by the ESF.

Rate of Return Analysis. Herrick (1989) presented an ex-post cost-benefit analysis of a small sample of the completed projects, commissioned by the Bank to gauge the investment impact of the ESF.

Macroeconomic Impact. In July 1989, the ESF commissioned a study of its macroeconomic impact (UDAPE, 1989). The study modeled the results of investment through the ESF compared to equal investment through traditional

surprisingly hard to do. Comparable quantitative measures of success are hard to find because the ESF had an unusual mix of emergency and development objectives and because it worked in several sectors. It cannot be compared fairly with straight infrastructure projects that have no labor intensity or poverty/targeting objectives. Nor is it completely fair to compare it to the Asian schemes that guaranchannels, and ESF investment together with other changes in the macroeconomy.

Institutional Impact. In July 1989, the ESF commissioned a study of its effect on the institutions with which it worked (SYSTEMA, 1989). A sample of organizations which had supervised, executed or been the beneficiaries of ESF projects was surveyed. The study focused on changes in institutional goals, procedures, capital stock, and activities.

Study of El Alto. The ESF contracted a study of the ESF's impact in El Alto, an impoverished suburb of La Paz where the ESF concentrated a large amount of its funding (CEDLA, 1989).

Political Impact. Graham (1991) examined the impact of politics on the ESF, and the ESF's impact on partisan politics.

Impact of Health and Nutrition Projects. Patino *et al.* visited 65 health and nutrition projects of all types in 1990. The study summarized their results and made suggestions about how the Social Investment Fund could improve on the ESF's record.

Bank Reviews

Geographic Targeting. VanDomelen (1989), using the ESF information system and UNDP poverty maps, analyzed the effectiveness of the ESF's project selection procedure in distributing project funds by geographic poverty ranking.

Country Economic Memorandum. The Country Economic Memorandum (Report No. 7645-BO), issued in September 1989, summarized the goals and results of the ESF in so far as information was then available.

Project Performance Audit Report on ESF I. When Credit 1829-BO closed, a project completion report was compiled, and the Operations Evaluation Department performed a project performance audit report.

Mid-Project Review of ESF II. Under the terms of Credit 1882-BO, ESF II, a mid-project review was completed in January 1989.

Procurement Reviews. Also under the terms of Credit 1882-BO, quarterly reviews of the ESF's procurement practices were performed by the Bank supervision team.

Supervision Reports. The Bank spent 78 staff weeks over two years supervising the first ESF project loan, Credit 1829-BO, more than twice the normal effort.

tee employment, but subordinate the infrastructure creation goals. In any case, the quantitative data on either class of potential comparator is fragmented and subject to a variety of technical and interpretive difficulties. Where possible, comparisons are presented here, but their occurrence is unsatisfyingly rare. For what it is worth, the author and many of those with whom she has discussed the ESF over the years would rate favorably the ESF's performance, given its goals. Critics of the ESF tend to fault its goals more than its performance in accomplishing them.

Administrative Efficiency

In seeking to fulfill its goal of cushioning the social impact of Bolivia's economic crisis, the ESF mobilized and invested large amounts of funding under difficult circumstances and in a relatively short period of time. (See Chapter 1 for a description of the project cycle and portfolio of the ESF.) This section looks in more depth at efficiency issues. Subsequent sections will discuss the impact that the ESF's expenditures had on various aspects of the Bolivian economy.

Administrative Costs

In the face of a workload of over 7,000 projects received and 3,000 approved, the ESF operated quickly and with low overhead. Administrative costs averaged about 3.5 percent of the total budget. The ESF built its staffing levels up gradually in response to growth in the workload. Once at full load, there were about 80 professional staff, and the entire staff complement, including support personnel, totalled approximately 130. The appraisal department, a critical component of the project cycle, approved as many as 20 to 30 projects a week valued at up to $2 million, with a staff of 12 to 15 persons.

The ESF's administrative costs as share of portfolio were slightly below those of other social funds modeled after it in Haiti, Honduras, and Guatemala. Their administrative costs ran from 6 to 10 percent. The Bolivian ESF's costs were about the same as the World Bank's which run from 3 to 4 percent. The ESF's record contrasted sharply with a project having a broadly similar mission, the Community Development Fund in the Ministry of Agriculture, that spent more than 50 percent of total cost on administration.

Cost Overruns

Cost overruns were minimal, averaging only about 3 percent of project commitments. However, the true size of cost overruns was not always fully counted. Most projects were, indeed, brought in at cost, but when cost overruns were large, the project scope would sometimes be cut back, or an ancillary but administratively separate project would be approved. By contrast, in the cases of cost underruns, the volume of work was frequently expanded to exhaust the available budget. In general, any divergence between estimated and actual cost was more often due to misestimation of physical volumes than of unit costs. (See Chapter 5 for a discussion of the ESF's unit cost system.)

Project Delays

The ESF calculated a rate of project delay as a measure of smooth implementation. The rate was defined as the percent of the work completed divided by the percent of the planned project execution period elapsed, subtracted from one.[1] The ESF considered a 40 percent rate acceptable. This relatively high figure was tolerated for the following reasons:

- the tendency to underestimate the time needed for project start-up;
- high turnover in project labor due to low wages;
- slow procurement of materials as contractors arrange purchases to comply with ESF unit prices; and
- changes in project design due to technical weaknesses in supervising agencies; and periodic inclement weather.

The rate of delay fluctuated over time, as shown in Table 3.1. Delays tended to be highest in the early period, as the ESF was still refining its project supervision procedures, and had not yet begun to feel the impact of a concerted effort to reduce delays that was started in July 1988. After that time, delays fell on average, though there was still significant fluctuation. Weather was always an important cause of this fluctuation. Occasionally other factors intervened. For example, immediately following the change in national government in August 1989, delays rose as staff in many soliciting and supervising agencies changed.

By way of comparison, a similarly calculated delay between disbursements as predicted at the time of appraisal and as occurring in practice showed that for projects in the World Bank's Latin America and Caribbean portfolio, the average lag was 20 percent.

Project Suspension

When projects encountered severe snags, funding (and work) would be suspended while solutions to the problem were sought. If the problems could be resolved, work was resumed. If not, the project was canceled. Problem projects were very

Table 3.1 Rate of Project Delays (percent)

1988		*1989*		*1990*	
May 15	68	June	44	April	47
June 16	76	November	57		
July 16	81				
August 17	74				
September 14	52				
October 20	50				
November 17	46				

Source: Procurement Review.

Table 3.2 Problem Projects Over Time

	8/88	*11/88*	*3/89*	*6/89*	*11/89*
Total Projects Approved	1,162	1,549	1,898	2,059	2,562
Total Projects in Execution	618	739	915	978	749
Under Temporary Suspension	1	4	18	44	11
In Process of Cancellation	2	0	4	12	16
Canceled	10	10	11	11	20

Source: Procurement Reviews.

few, as shown in Table 3.2. Project cancellations typically accounted for well under one percent of the number of approved projects. Serious problems ran the gamut from lack of counterpart funds and land tenure disputes to noncompliance of the contractor with the terms of his contract. No one single type of major problem appears to have predominated.

Technical Quality of Works

In 1988, strong concerns arose that the technical quality of the physical works was so low as to jeopardize their value. Indeed, this is an issue that has never entirely been put to rest among the ESF's critics. The concerns were not without substance in some cases. The ESF hired an independent engineer to audit technical quality and followed his recommendations where quality was found to be substandard. Overall, project quality was found to be acceptable.

The quality ratings as determined in the above-mentioned audit for a sample of 186 projects are shown in Table 3.3. Although the projects audited were not a randomly chosen sample of the ESF's portfolio, it is interesting to make a few observations on them. First, rural projects were apparently as well executed as were urban projects. Concerns about difficulties for supervision teams in gaining access to remote areas, and about a lack of institutional capacity for project management and implementation in rural areas were thus not borne out by the survey. Second, projects sponsored by non-governmental organizations (NGOs) had technical quality ratings equal to the overall average. The limited experience of many NGOs in matters of construction seems to have been overcome adequately in supervision arrangements. Regional development corporations (RDCs), on the other hand, were generally thought to have the best technical capacity for project formulation and supervision. Why they should have been the sponsoring agency with the worst average technical quality rating for projects completed is unclear. It may be that for RDCs, only known problem projects were audited. Third, urban improvement projects had the poorest quality rating of all project types. These were largely street paving projects, which formed a disproportionate share of the ESF's early portfolio. Their low quality could have been the result of growing pains in ESF

Table 3.3 Average Quality Rating by Project Features

	Number of Projects	*Average Rating*
Overall Average	186	1.9
Location		
Rural	36	2.0
Urban	150	1.9
Sponsoring Agency		
Regional Development Corporation	13	2.2
Municipalities	33	2.0
CONES	23	1.9
National Road Service	4	1.3
Other governmental	62	1.7
NGOs	53	1.9
Project Type		
Social Infrastructure	142	1.8
Water & Sewerage	24	1.7
Housing	20	1.6
Health Infrastructure	14	1.9
Schools	50	2.0
Historical Renovations	5	1.4
Other	5	2.2
Orphanages/Old Folks Homes	18	1.8
Other Education Construction	6	2.0
Economic Infrastructure	44	2.0
Urban Improvements (paving, markets)	26	2.4
Access Roads	7	1.6
Irrigation	1	1.0
Drainage	2	1.0
Erosion Control/Reforestation	6	1.5
Others	2	1.5

Ratings: 1 = Good, 2 = Acceptable, 3 = Deficient, 4 = Poor

Source: Technical Audits

project selection and supervision capability, or of several problems in getting adequate materials.

The ESF managed to appraise, finance, and monitor the implementation of thousands of small development projects. This was no mean feat given the prevailing public sector climate in Bolivia, where, typically, only about 50 percent of planned public investments came to fruition. Having established that the ESF did indeed generate a remarkable amount of investment activity, it remains to consider, in the remaining sections, the impact of the ESF.

Targeting

Targeting Tools

As originally conceived, the ESF's main benefit was to be the wages paid to laborers on ESF-financed projects. Targeting for those benefits occurred through self-selection: the wage offered at ESF projects was set at a rate likely to attract poor laborers, i.e., the market wage for heavy, unskilled manual labor. A decision not to offer below market wages (which should ensure strict self-targeting) was made by the ESF's designers for four reasons. First, the introduction of market signals was fundamental to the adjustment program, and the designers wished to extend the principle to the ESF as well. Second, there was concern that if the ESF paid below market wages, workers might be poorly motivated, leading to problems with the supervision and quality of works. Thus finer targeting could have had high costs in administration and loss of investment impact. Third, below market wages would not transfer sufficient income to the workers, thereby negating the program's goals. Fourth, even at market rates, the type of work offered paid wages that were low enough to ensure fairly good targeting.

In contrast to the primacy of wage benefits, the benefits of the infrastructure created were viewed, at least in the early stages of the ESF, as being secondary. Targeting for infrastructure benefits was achieved by selecting types of projects likely to benefit the poor (e.g., provision of water and sewerage in small towns and slums, upgrading of rural feeder roads, repairs of public schools) and, in most categories of projects, by funding project proposals received from poorer areas.

Outcome: Targeting of Employment Benefits

Data on ESF workers and their characteristics were analyzed most completely by Newman, Jorgensen, and Pradhan (see Chapter 4). Their findings indicated that the typical ESF worker was male, married, head of his household, and the sole income-earner in the family. He had received less formal education than males in the general population, and his family spent less on food per household member than did families in the general population. Newman, Jorgensen and Pradhan's model predicted that if the ESF's workers were in the general labor market, 77 percent of them would have been in the poorest 40 percent of the income distribution.

By way of contrast, two poverty alleviation programs that use a very different mechanism, but for which incidence was well studied, are the Sri Lankan and Jamaican food stamps programs. Sixty-one and 56 percent of benefits, respectively, accrued to the poorest 40 percent of households (Edirisinghe (1987) and Grosh (1990a)). A review of the incidence of public primary health and public primary education expenditures in Latin America (Grosh, 1990b), showed the share accruing to the poorest 40 percent of the population to range from 15-60 for education and from 30-70 for health.

Ravallion (1991), summarized the targeting performance of two Asian employment programs. Both focused much more heavily than the ESF on providing improvements to welfare through wages, giving little weight to the return to the infrastructure or the physical quality of the work. Both used below market wages, and both used government agencies to carry out the works. These differences, however, do not seem unduly large. For Bangladesh's Food for Work Program, 70 percent of days of employment went to the poorest 25 percent of rural households. For the Maharastra (India) Employment Guarantee Scheme, about 90 percent of EGS workers were below the poverty line (including their EGS-generated income) whereas the average figure for rural Maharastra was more on the order of 50 percent.

The targeting of ESF wage benefits fell within the range of other social welfare programs—better than some and worse than others.

Outcome: Targeting of Project Benefits

Information on beneficiaries of completed projects was scant; geographic distribution was used as a proxy for poverty targeting of beneficiaries of ESF projects. Geographic targeting was a simple way of giving preference to particular areas, and thereby, to groups whose socio-economic characteristics might correlate highly with their location. For example, people living in slums are poor, poverty rates are usually higher in rural areas than in urban areas, and so on.

The ESF set goals for the distribution of project funds to each of Bolivia's nine administrative departments. The goals were based on the proportion of the national population in each department and were adjusted for regional income per capita, unemployment, infant mortality, school attendance, and other indicators. As of August 31, 1988, actual allocations differed from programmed allocations by no more than 0.3 percent. Thus, at the departmental level, geographic targeting was quite good.

Because there was a great deal of variability in welfare levels within areas as large as Bolivia's departments, it was important to use finer geographic distinctions. Accordingly, VanDomelen (1989) calculated geographical targeting by province, the finest level of detail then available for regional characteristics. There are 99 provinces in Bolivia, classified into 5 poverty levels by the Ministry of Planning on the basis of data on infant mortality, social services, education, economic production, access to infrastructure, and so on, based on the 1976 census. Both the classification scheme and the data on which it is based are old, but remain the best available tools for poverty mapping.

Table 3.4 gives a breakdown of ESF funds committed by poverty area as of March 1989.[2] Per capita expenditures were regressively distributed, with Area 1, the least poor, obtaining $23.97 per capita in ESF commitments, and Area 5, the poorest, receiving $9.45 per capita. In interpreting results, it should be remem-

Table 3.4 Distribution of ESF Commitments by Poverty Area as of March 1989

Poverty Area	1985 Population (millions)	ESF Commitments Total (millions)	ESF Commitments Per Capita	Approval Rate[a] (percent)
1 (least poor)	2.3	$56.1	$23.97	24
2	.7	20.3	27.77	23
3	1.3	17.3	13.51	25
4	1.4	16.3	11.67	33
5 (poorest)	.6	6.2	9.45	28
National	6.4	116.1	18.20	25

a. The ratio of approved to solicited funding.
Source: VanDomelen (1989).

bered that even data gathered at the provincial level mask large disparities in the standard of living, particularly in urban areas. For example, Poverty Area 1 included only departmental capitals, and in these cities ESF projects were frequently in the poorest areas. It is therefore possible that ESF projects were reaching pockets of poverty within generally better-off provinces.

The last column in Table 3.4 gives the ratio of approved to solicited funding. Without some objective measure of the quality of proposed projects, it is difficult to say whether the ESF accepted lower quality projects in the poorest areas in order to improve targeting. These numbers do not suggest a strong bias toward accepting projects in poor areas. Anecdotal evidence suggests that the ESF promotion staff spent extra time helping agencies in poor areas bring their proposals up to acceptable quality.

The approximately constant project approval rates across poverty areas and the regressive distribution of benefits underlined the difficulties of targeting in a demand-driven institution such as the ESF (see Chapter 7). Typically, the poorest communities were also those with the weakest institutions and the poorest channels of communication with the rest of the country, factors that were critical in determining both the capacity of a community to participate in a program such as the ESF, and the likelihood that the community would be interested in participating in the first place. The lack of government and NGO presence in many of the most needy areas of Bolivia has meant that intermediaries were not available for help in organizing project proposals. The ESF's promotion unit met with some success in increasing the flow of good-quality project proposals from poorer regions. In October 1987, the difference in per capita expenditures between the poorest and richest poverty areas was on the order of four to one (Castaños, *et. al.*). By July 1989, the difference was reduced to three to one.

Impact on Incomes

By mid-1990, more than 20,000 people were working at projects funded by the ESF. Newman, Jorgensen and Pradhan, (see Chapter 4), estimated that 18 percent of persons employed at ESF-funded projects would have been unemployed were it not for the ESF. If, at first glance, this should seem to be a rather low figure, indicating that the ESF was only moderately successful in alleviating "unemployment" caused by the economic crisis, it must be remembered that true unemployment in Bolivia was rather low, given the absence of unemployment insurance or welfare benefits. Few heads of household could afford not to be engaged in some form of economic activity—in the informal, if not the formal sector—even if the pay was quite low. Thus it becomes more meaningful to look at how well the ESF reduced underemployment, as opposed to unemployment. In this regard, Newman, Jorgensen and Pradhan have shown that the average ESF worker had weekly earnings that were 49 percent higher than they would have been had that worker in fact been able to find work in the absence of the ESF, and 67 percent higher than such worker's earnings would be on average, when considering that some would be unemployed.

Alternately expressed, forgone income of ESF workers was about 60 percent of the wages received. This was slightly higher than the two Asian schemes referred to earlier. For the Maharastra scheme, an upper bound on the comparable figure was 53 percent, for Bangladesh it was 57 percent (Ravallion, 1991). Given that both the Asian programs use below market wages, it was surprising that the percent of foregone income was in the same range.

Using a general equilibrium model, UDAPE (1988) calculated that every job created by the ESF resulted in the creation of another 1.1 jobs in the Bolivian economy. This multiplier effect was attributable mainly to the low import content of inputs used at ESF-financed projects. From a microeconomic perspective, Newman, Jorgensen and Pradhan did not find any effect of the ESF on the wage of the general labor market. A similar result was found by UDAPE.

Investment Impact

As part of its project appraisal process, the ESF calculated rough internal rates of return for proposed infrastructure projects. A sample of these by project type is presented in Table 3.5. The overall average projected rate of return for approved projects was 22 percent, a figure that, if reasonably close to the mark, suggests that these projects created infrastructure that contributed substantial long-term benefits.

Some confirmation of the ESF's rate-of-return projections was provided by Herrick (1989), who conducted after-the-fact cost benefit analyses on 20 projects. His sample was not completely random because he had to rely on the ESF staff's advice on the physical accessibility of projects and the availability of sound data.

Table 3.5 Ex-Ante Rates of Return of ESF Projects

Project Type	*Average Rate of Return (percent)*
Road Improvement	24
Housing	22
Street Paving	15
Sewerage	21
Potable Water	22
Irrigation	30
Weighted Average	22

Source: ESF.

The sample would appear, nonetheless, to be reasonably representative within each type of project evaluated. Herrick's calculations were based on a simplified method in which benefits and maintenance costs were assumed to be capitalized in the value of the residential property served by the water, sewerage and street paving projects he evaluated.

Of the twenty projects Herrick evaluated, three had total costs greater than their benefits (i.e., the cost-benefit ratio was less than one; see Table 3.6), and two just broke even. All the remaining fifteen were sound investments; 10 had benefits equal to more than four times their costs.

Herrick performed sensitivity analyses to see how greatly his results would change if the change in property values caused by ESF works was different from that projected. In general, he found that even if property values increased much less than projected, the projects would remain profitable.

In interpreting the cost-benefit ratios, it should be kept in mind that project selection criteria included both the economic rate of return and poverty targeting. These two factors are, however, generally opposed, as the economic return on improvements in wealthy neighborhoods would in most cases be greater than that in poor neighborhoods. This makes it all the more remarkable that economic returns of ESF projects were generally positive.

The Impact of Health and Nutrition Projects

Patiño *et al.*'s review of the ESF's health and nutrition projects reveals much of the difficulty of evaluating the ESF. The study was commissioned to improve on the procedures not for the ESF, but for its successor organization, the Social Investment Fund (see Chapter 9).

A multidisciplinary team visited 65 projects, which accounted for about half of the amount spent on health and nutrition projects. A scoring system was used which graded projects on thirteen different indicators of impact and quality of implementation[3]. The project was assigned an overall score that was the average

Table 3.6 Herrick's Benefit-Cost Ratios

Project	Benefit-Cost Ratio	Rate of Increase of Property Values (%): Observed	Rate of Increase of Property Values (%): Necessary to Cover Total Costs[a]
Street Paving			
1	0.99	30	30
2	2.03	81	40
3	0.88	40	45
4	4.91	67	14
5	22.74	63	3
6	5.88	28	5
7	5.03	33	7
8	8.12	35	4
9	5.54	n.a.	n.a.
10	8.76	14	2
11	2.25	67	30
Sewers			
1	0.99	25	25
2	2.56	35	14
3	1.52	78	52
4	1.73	20	12
5	0.84	33	40
6	4.19	53	13
Water			
1	0.92	40	44
2	4.47	33	7
3	4.76	75	16

a. Note on interpretation. Example: Paving project No. 2. Observed property value increased by 80 percent, but an increase of 40 percent would have been enough to cover the total project costs (at shadow prices), while an increase of only 21 percent would have covered the ESF's costs (also at shadow prices).

Source: Herrick (1989), Tables 5 and 6.

from the separate indicators. In addition, a good deal of qualitative information was gathered.

In all, 51 percent of the health and nutrition projects evaluated were judged to be of good quality, 32 percent were rated fair, and 16 percent were rated as poor. Day care centers rated uniformly as good. Projects which provided integrated primary health care also rated well. All the nutrition projects rated good, except for school breakfast projects, which were generally fair. Projects which concentrated on building new health infrastructure fared worst, with problems in staffing and running the health posts or centers constructed.

It was not possible to determine precisely the impact of ESF-financed projects on health or nutrition indicators. It is inherently very difficult to do because each project had such a small area of influence that extremely disaggregated data would be necessary. Furthermore, the ESF financing usually improved the quality, range or coverage of services offered by existing programs. Changes in health or nutrition status were due not only to the part of the services financed by the ESF, but by the complimentary actions of the implementing agency. The ESF did not have a system in place to overcome these difficulties to monitor the impact of its projects on health and nutrition. Rather it financed only services that had been shown to have positive impacts in other circumstances and presumed that if the actions were carried out satisfactorily, health improvements would occur.

The Patiño study refers to two sets of evidence that suggest the benefit of some of the ESF's health and nutrition projects. A few of the NGOs that were the main providers of health services in their regions kept very detailed health statistics. These NGOs showed that the infant mortality rate fell markedly (in some cases by half) in the few years they have operated. The ESF provided financing to expand the coverage of these programs. There is little doubt that those projects had a health impact, but it is impossible to measure it precisely.

A second suggestion of the impact of the health and nutrition projects is that the prevalence of malnutrition as reported by the nutrition surveillance system has decreased from about 60 percent to 40 percent.[4]

The study's criticisms of projects were similar to criticisms of health interventions financed by or carried out by other actors in the health sector in Bolivia, which was unsurprising since the ESF merely increased other actors' resources. The criticisms related to the adequacy of staff and supplies in relation to infrastructure, the low quality of some infrastructure, the emphasis on curative care, the inadequacy of some medical personnel's ability to deal with the target population, the frequency with which health posts were closed, the questionable sustainability of projects, etc. The concerns were real, and the effectiveness of the portfolio was lower than ideal. Better project promotion, appraisal and supervision procedures by the ESF might have been able to raise the quality of the portfolio. The extent to which that would have been possible was limited by the prevailing quality of health interventions which formed the pool of project proposals among which the ESF chose.

There was no comparison made with the quality of projects financed from other sources, so it is difficult to judge from the study whether having provided the money to the health sector through a mechanism other than the ESF would have given better results. The Ministry of Health projects, in general, were found to be less good than those of religious NGOs, but better than those of non-religious NGOs.

The interpretation of the Patiño study depends upon the perspective from which it is viewed. If the question is "did the ESF help improve health and nutrition in Bolivia?", the answer is yes. If the question is "were there flaws in the ESF program?" the answer is also yes. Having 51 percent of the projects rated as good can be compared to having a glass half full of milk. Some call it half full, and some call it half empty. When the ESF was put together, the glass was perceived as being empty so that a half full glass was a marked improvement. As the ESF evolved and the economic crisis abated, sights were raised and the glass began to seem half empty.

Macroeconomic Impact

An internal World Bank report prepared in 1989 estimated that projected disbursements by the ESF of $100 million in that year were equal to about 30 percent of the public sector investment program executed through traditional channels. Conservatively, the report calculated that the $100 million would generate an increase in GDP of about 2.0 percent.[5] Scaling this calculation down to the actual amount of ESF disbursements in 1989, $66 million, gives an estimate of GDP growth attributable to the ESF of 1.3 percent.

A rather more detailed analysis of the ESF's macroeconomic impact was found in UDAPE (1989). UDAPE used a general equilibrium model calibrated to represent the structure of the economy in 1987, when the ESF was founded. The model consisted of nine productive sectors, the government, the financial sector, four social groups (peasants, salaried workers, informal sector workers and capitalists) and a residual sector. The model had 49 exogenous and 276 endogenous variables.

UDAPE compared two simulation scenarios: (a) the cumulative effect of ESF's activities in 1987, 1988, and the first half of 1989; and (b) the effect of an equal amount of resources invested through traditional channels. ESF activities were characterized as changes in four aggregates. Disbursements for economic and social infrastructure projects contributed to the construction sector; disbursements for social assistance projects and ESF operating expenses contributed to government expenditures; productive projects contributed to credit; and about 4 percent of the total went to import capital goods. In case b, an equal amount of resources were channeled through public enterprises, the government, and to a lesser extent, the financial system.

Investment through the ESF generally showed better results than investment through traditional channels would have. In case a, the ESF case, GDP grew by 2.5 percent, inflation rose by 1.7 percent and employment increased by 57,000 jobs. In case b, with investment through traditional channels, GDP grew by 2 percent, inflation rose by 1.9 percent and 45,000 jobs were created.

UDAPE tried to evaluate the long term growth implications of investment through the ESF versus normal channels. The model calculated that an additional dollar of foreign resource mobilization spent through the ESF would increase investment by $.86, while if invested through traditional channels, would increase investment by $.70. Thus investment through the ESF was preferred on the grounds of efficiency.[6]

Institutional Impact

By March of 1989, the ESF had worked with about 550 different organizations in the public, private and voluntary sectors. Four-fifths of these organizations were NGOs, which accounted for about a third of the dollar value of approved projects. One indication of the ESF's impact was the effect it had on the capacity of local organizations to design project proposals. In the early days of the ESF, only one in ten projects received were well enough formulated to be appraised. By late 1988, eight of ten projects received were appraisable. Other indicators were anecdotal or less tangible, e.g., the passage of the NGO community from complete unwillingness to work with the ESF, to a fairly widespread agreement to work together constructively on practical matters and to disagree peacefully on some political issues. As the awareness of its impact on collaborating institutions grew, the ESF commissioned a study on the subject.

SYSTEMA (1989) considered two types of effects. The first was called "Institutional Level," which covered effects that might be felt well beyond the work on a specific ESF-financed project, i.e., that would affect the rest of the institutions' activities. Managers were asked to specify the ESF's impact on their organizations' goals, procedures, infrastructure and finances. The second set of effects were at the "Project Level," being more closely linked with the implementation and supervision of specific projects. Project-level effects were divided into technical processes, personnel, and inter-organizational coordination.

Positive impact at the institutional level was reported by 80 percent of state agencies and 60 percent of NGOs (for more on the impact of NGOs, see Chapter 6). The impact was largest under the following circumstances: ESF financing was a large part of the portfolio; the institutions were in the process of reorganization and had many unmet demands, as in the case of several municipalities; the agency had broad contacts with the community it served and other organizations; and the agency had a clearly defined purpose and ambitious goals for population coverage. The impact tended to be small in organizations with the following characteristics: those that served as project supervisors rather than the agency requesting project funding; those with large portfolios of ongoing works such as the regional development corporations and the large, national NGOs; those with a vertical, closed organizational structure characteristic of many state agencies and religious NGOs.

In most cases, the most important impact of the ESF funding was to enable the institutions to fulfill better existing goals. Services offered to existing target populations were improved or complementary services offered, rather than target populations being expanded. Procedures were changed, mostly in financial administration, in a third of cases. About a fifth of the organizations expanded, reorganized or updated their infrastructure.

At the project level, working with the ESF was found to have a positive impact on planning, feasibility studies and, to a lesser extent, on project supervision. Little impact on personnel was noted in the state agencies. For those, three quarters of staff working on ESF projects held the same job, with substantially the same duties after involvement with the ESF as before. In NGOs, on the other hand, almost half of the personnel involved with ESF projects were promoted or newly contracted.

While it remains difficult to define and measure the impact of the ESF on the institutions with which it worked, SYSTEMA's study did confirm a widely spread and positive impact. SYSTEMA did suggest, however, that the permanency of some aspects was tenuous.

The Political Sustainability of the Adjustment Program

It was difficult to establish any direct or casual relationship between the ESF and the political substainability of the macroeconomic adjustment program. In seeking to understand the issue, Molina Rivera, *et. al.* (1988) and Graham (1991) provided some insights into the ESF's popular image and the impact this had on the tolerance for the adjustment program.

ESF's Popular Image

The ESF commissioned an anthropological study (Molino Rivera *et. al.* (1988)), conducted from April through September 1988, to learn how ESF projects were affecting the communities and how the ESF was perceived by the beneficiaries. In Castaños, *et al.* (1988), there was also some information gained as to workers' perceptions of the ESF, and CEDLA (1989) contained findings on beneficiary perceptions of ESF. These results are the most concrete way of approaching the issue of popular impact. Unless otherwise noted, the results presented here are from Molino Rivera, *et. al.* In discussing the ESF's popular image, it is convenient to consider separately various groups, especially workers on ESF projects, communities which benefitted from the infrastructure and services provided by ESF projects, and the contractors.

Workers. Well over half of the 249 workers interviewed expressed satisfaction with the ESF-generated employment, largely for want of any other source of income. As one worker stated:

> "They pay us little, but worse is nothing; what else can we do? One has to take home a little money and there are no jobs..." (p.22)

The most frequently held prior occupation was in construction (44 percent), which may well explain why close to half (47 percent) of the workers said they had learned nothing new in their ESF project work. Yet, even with the other half having learned something new, over two thirds of the workers were apprehensive about finding work after the termination of the ESF project. On balance, the workers on ESF projects were glad to have a job, but concerned about its low pay and temporary nature, and about their prospects for future employment.

The benefit to the government of this generally satisfactory reaction by ESF workers was diminished by ignorance on the part of those workers as to what the ESF was, and that it was financing their salaries. In the 1988 study, only 29 percent knew approximately what ESF was.

Beneficiaries. In the case of infrastructure projects, 80 percent of community residents interviewed felt they had benefitted greatly from the ESF project and that "the works were a need very much felt by the community" (p.30). About half of the beneficiaries living in communities receiving ESF infrastructure projects actively participated in the project design or execution, and a third thought that the work on the projects had strengthened their community organizations.

In contrast to the case of the laborers hired on ESF projects, three quarters of the beneficiaries of infrastructure projects knew something of the ESF, at least with reference to their specific project.

In the case of social assistance projects, three quarters of the beneficiaries thought that the projects were important both to their families and to the community in general. A like proportion said that the community, through its various organizations, had been involved in the design and implementation of the projects. Those who felt the projects were not useful usually cited the temporary nature of the funding, especially in the nutrition projects.

Only sixty percent of beneficiaries of the social assistance projects realized that the benefits were due to ESF financing.

Anecdotal evidence from Bank supervision missions and ESF project supervisors confirmed that beneficiaries were in general pleased with their projects. Indeed, a recurring theme in conversations with beneficiaries was that their experience with ESF projects was the first time they had ever perceived the government to be doing something to their benefit.

Contractors. In the case of infrastructure projects, the study interviewed the contractors responsible for carrying out the works. Eighty percent of the contractors said that ESF contracts had been economically important for them, given the depression in the construction market. Nonetheless, when asked whether they had problems with the ESF, 60 percent of contractors responded affirmatively, mentioning most frequently the low (in their opinion) unit costs fixed by the ESF. Sixty-one percent of the implementing agencies were private firms, of which a third were operating nationally. For about half the firms, ESF projects were apparently an important source of income. In the case of social assistance projects, 70 percent of the implementing agencies were pleased with the results of the projects. Of those who cited problems, they were again related to the temporary nature of the nutrition projects, and sometimes to the controversy surrounding food donations.

Implementing Agencies. ESF-financed projects were carried out by a variety of agencies, most of which (especially NGOs and municipal governments) were not part of the central government and could, therefore, oppose it. With these groups, the ESF was largely successful. In spite of a few highly visible failures, the ESF was able to improve NGO-government relations and provide a workable mechanism for cooperation at the technical level, even when political differences were present. Municipal governments were, by and large, willing to work with the ESF because the municipal government could easily present itself as the party responsible for the benefits from the works it carried out with ESF financing (Graham, 1991).

From Popular Image to Political Sustainability

Graham (1991), after reviewing the ESF's relationships with NGOs, municipalities, and electoral politics, draws two conclusions germane here. First, the generally satisfactory view of the ESF by its workers, beneficiaries, and implementing agencies helped sustain the adjustment process. The large scale of the program strengthened the impact, which was tempered by the lack of familiarity with the program by many of its beneficiaries.

> The *perception* that the government is doing something to make the adjustment process less painful or costly is important to the political process of sustaining adjustment. Whether this support is for the adjustment process *per se* or for the government implementing it is not necessarily a relevant distinction. In the case of the ESF, unprecedented numbers of poor were reached, and local organizations and governments established a cooperative working relationship with the government for the first time. Groups that traditionally had been in opposition discovered that they could actually benefit from working with the government. If this did not create direct support, it at least reduced potential opposition to the government and its program. (p. 38)

There is a further conclusion relevant to those who seek to replicate the ESF in other countries:

> The ESF did not build support for the government among the sectors most directly affected by the adjustment program — the miners in particular, but instead among large numbers of the nation's poor that had been previously neglected by the state. This strategy was successful because in numerical terms the miners were a minority, and because the ESF had sufficient financial resources to reach a number of poor that was significant relative to Bolivia's total population. In a nation where the organized base of opposition was relatively larger, or where resources were more limited, the political dynamic might not be the same, and the issue of who the program targeted might have to take very different criteria into account, if contributing to the political sustainability of adjustment was a major goal of the compensation program.

Lessons

Implicit in the studies reviewed here are several lessons for those considering the establishment of similar organizations.[7] These are enumerated briefly in this final section.

Administration Is a Worthwhile Investment. Attempts are being made to emulate the ESF in other developing countries largely because it was successful in efficiently managing a large number of projects and channelling what, for Bolivia, was a large sum of money from external donors to local development organizations. It could not have achieved this without excellent management, high caliber staff, a sophisticated management information system, and a full complement of office technology (computers, photocopiers, facsimile machines, two way radios, etc.).

An ESF Should Finance, but Not Formulate or Implement Projects. The ESF catalyzed dramatic numbers of projects by providing a source of funds with relatively simple procedures for applications. The detailed work of project formulation and implementation was left to the soliciting and supervising agencies that supplied untold person-years of labor in the effort. Had the ESF tried to take on that burden, its staff would have had to be several times larger, and the number of completed projects a fraction as many.

Short-cut Targeting Goes a Long Way. The ESF's targeting mechanisms, shaped by a need to act as quickly as possible, were simple and crude. By offering market wages in a low income sector, ESF automatically attracted workers who were predominantly poor, if not the poorest of the poor. Similarly, in targeting the benefits of the infrastructure created and services provided by projects, the level of sophistication rarely went beyond attempting to ensure that the project would be located in a poor neighborhood, or that it would provide something more likely to be in demand among the poor than among the better-off. These mechanisms were not sufficient to assure fine targeting, but accomplished a good deal. Most of the beneficiaries, both in the short run and in the long run, were poor.

Short-cut Project Evaluation Goes a Long Way. The ESF's project appraisal procedures were designed more for speed than for accuracy. Further, they were designed more to cull out projects that did not pass a minimum threshold of acceptability than to establish priorities within groups of acceptable projects. Nonetheless, the procedures used were sufficient to select a generally high return portfolio of projects.

Trade-offs Must Be Made Between the Quality and Size of Portfolio. Clearly there was room for improving the ESF's targeting, evaluation, and supervision procedures, but improvement would have come at the expense of slower turnaround of project proposals, higher overhead, and ultimately, fewer completed projects. In the ESF's case this was deemed too high a price. In other situations it may be more appropriate to pay that price. In Bolivia, the ESF's successor organization, the Social Investment Fund, will work on upgrading the rough-and-ready targeting, appraisal and supervision procedures used by the ESF as it focuses on long-term development in health and education.

Employment Projects Can Create Useful Infrastructure. Employment projects, including the ESF, are sometimes treated as though their only benefit is the immediate benefit to workers that result from the wages they are paid. In fact, the ESF also showed that high return infrastructure can be built in an employment project. The infrastructure's long run benefits should be considered in addition to workers' income gains.

Project Outreach (Promotion) Is Necessary. Even with a plethora of unmet demands and of eligible institutions, special efforts were necessary to disseminate information on the ESF, its goals and procedures, and to build confidence in its ability to deal fairly and promptly with the soliciting agencies. Similar institutions that choose to model themselves after the ESF should build this process in from the beginning and plan a slow initial phase until the demand for projects is mobilized.

A Pilot Demonstration Is Effective. In its search for external financing, ESF started operations with a commitment of only $10 million, a fraction of its investment goal of $180 million. As the ESF demonstrated through its operations that it could absorb and use well large quantities of resources, additional commitments from a number of donors, as well as a second World Bank credit became available. In the end, the ESF surpassed its goal of a portfolio of $180 million. The ESF also used the project's pilot demonstration effect in wooing implementing agencies, especially NGOs. Faced with an initial scarcity of goodwill and project submissions from NGOs, the ESF funded a few, demonstrated the advantages of working with the ESF, and gradually won the confidence of a broad spectrum of agencies.

Special Public Relations Efforts May Be Needed for a Financial Intermediary to Get Credit for the Works It Finances. The ESF financed works implemented by other agencies. Thus credit for the employment and services it paid for frequently went to the implementing agencies. If recognition of the financing agency itself is a goal, special attention needs be paid to ensuring that beneficiaries understand who is actually footing the bill. This will not be important in all cases, but if, for example, the government wishes to gain political tolerance for an adjustment program, it may not only need to fund an ESF-type program, but publicize that it is doing so, and its compensatory purpose.

An Institutional Multiplier Effect Is Possible. By virtue of having worked with the ESF, a significant number of agencies apparently improved their ability to do their other work well. In this, the simple, replicable, and yet detailed project submission procedures and the monitoring role of the Promotion Department were important.

There Need Not Be a Trade-Off between Short-Term Action and Long-Run Growth. In the case of the ESF, the macroeconomic analyses show that it fostered GDP growth in both the short run and long run. Contributing factors to this outcome were the short-run boost to demand, the investment value of infrastructure created, the higher elasticity of investment through ESF than through other channels, and the extent to which the ESF helped mobilize incremental foreign financing.

Notes

1. Take, for example, a $100,000 project that was to require 50 days to execute. After 25 days in execution, if $50,000 were disbursed, then the delay would be zero. The work was

50 percent complete, and 50 percent of the planned execution period had elapsed (i.e., 1-(50%/50%) =0). If after 25 days in execution, $25,000 were disbursed then the delay would be 50 percent. The work was 25 percent complete, and 50 percent of the planned execution period had elapsed (i.e., 1-(25%/50%) =.5).

2. See Chapter 6 for more detail on geographic poverty targeting by type of soliciting agency.

3. These were: that the project met a real health need of the target population; cost effectiveness; whether immunization services were regularly programmed or part of mass campaigns; the quality of the oral rehydration program; the improvement in nutritional status, diet, or nutrition knowledge of beneficiaries; quality of health education programs; quality of eradication of endemic problems or basic sanitation; health statistics; community relations; method and logistics of field work; experience of the implementing agency; capability of professional and technical staff; and compliance with project objectives.

4. The study does not specify all the relevant details. It appears that the figure refers to the incidence of low weight for age, including Gomez grades I-III. It is not stated what age group is included.

5. It is generally accepted that most of the external funding attracted by the ESF was incremental; that is, it was on top of what donors would have provided without the ESF.

6. UDAPE also calculated a third case which combined ESF investment with realistic macroeconomic changes such as the devaluation, trade deficit, drop in natural gas prices, etc. Outcomes were considerably less positive. GDP grew by only 1.4 percent, inflation rose 21.4 percent, and job growth was 42,000. An additional dollar of foreign resource mobilization would increase investment by only $.53. UDAPE thereby concluded that the ESF was an ineffectual investment channel and would hinder long term growth. Case 3 was included in order to provide a comparison between the model's predictions and observed outcomes in 1989. The inclusion of macroeconomic changes made it incomparable to either Case 1 or Case 2. The conclusion that investment through the ESF lowers growth was therefore unwarranted.

7. The lessons presented here are not all of the lessons from the ESF's experience, but rather are those which derive from the studies reviewed in this chapter.

4

How Did Workers Benefit?[1]

by John Newman, Steen Jorgensen,
and Menno Pradhan

This chapter presents estimates of the effect of the Emergency Social Fund (ESF) on employment and income of workers in ESF-financed projects, and on the urban labor market in general. This corresponds to estimating only one of the intended benefits of the ESF. It is important to recognize the additional objectives of the program—to generate productive economic infrastructure and to generate and disburse funds quickly. These objectives imposed constraints on the type of employment generation and income maintenance that were undertaken.

The first part of the chapter describes the characteristics of workers in ESF infrastructure projects and compares these workers to the urban population in general and to workers in the construction sector in particular. The second part of the chapter contains a counterfactual simulation, asking what would have been the position of the workers in the absence of the ESF program. Based on this simulation, inferences are made about the employment and income effect of the ESF program on the workers employed.

The *conclusions* are that the workers in ESF-funded urban infrastructure projects were mainly married, male, and heads of households. Seventy-seven percent of workers would have been among the 40 percent poorest had they *not* had the ESF-sponsored employment. The ESF job raised expected income by 67 percent on average and raised income more for the poorer groups.

The Data

Information on the general population was obtained from the 1988 Permanent Household Survey (EPH), part of an ongoing survey effort that has been conducted yearly by the National Institute of Statistics (INE) since 1976. The 1988 EPH took place in May and covered urban households in the capital cities of seven of Bolivia's nine administrative units (the departments). Information on workers and their families in ESF-funded projects was obtained from a special survey conducted for the ESF by INE. From a list of all ESF projects in execution, INE selected all those that were: (a) in capital cities, (b) in operation at the time of the EPH Survey, and (c) in economic infrastructure (i.e., explicitly employment generating). Only capital cities were chosen because INE's May 1988 household survey covers only the capitals and information on a control group was required for the analysis. A total of 64 projects met the requirements. INE then visited the projects to ascertain the actual number of workers employed at the projects and drew a random sample of 600 workers from the list of all workers. The ESF workers were visited in their homes and were given the same household questionnaire used in the broad EPH sample.

This procedure of conducting a separate sample of ESF workers was done for two reasons. First, at the time of the survey the size of the ESF program was small compared to the total economically active population, making it unlikely to find a sample of workers in the ESF in the general population that was large enough for analytical purposes.[2] Second, previous pilot surveys indicated that many of the workers who were actually working in ESF-financed projects did not know that they were doing so. This was confirmed by the fact that when INE visited workers known to work in the projects, having obtained their names and addresses from the subcontractors, a majority of the workers had not heard of the ESF. This meant that the only way of guaranteeing that ESF workers would be interviewed was to employ a separate sample consisting only of ESF workers.

Descriptive Statistics—ESF and Other Workers Compared

Background of ESF Workers

The workers in the sampled ESF projects were, for the most part, prime-age married males and were generally the head of their household. Ninety-nine percent were male and 71 percent were married. Ninety-one percent fell between the ages of 20 and 65 years old, and 93 percent reported themselves as head of household. These workers were apparently the prime income earners of their household and the earnings from the ESF projects were their primary source of income. In 62 percent of the households of ESF workers there was only one reported income earner, in 25 percent there were two, and in nine percent there were three. These results closely approximated the pattern of the 1987 survey. Only 7.2 percent of the ESF workers had a secondary job. This profile of ESF workers closely mirrors that of the construction sector as a whole. Very few women, and old and young men work in this sector.

In comparison with other workers in the construction sector, ESF workers were less educated. The distribution over the different education levels is given in Table 4.1.

Figure 4.1 Employment Position Prior to ESF

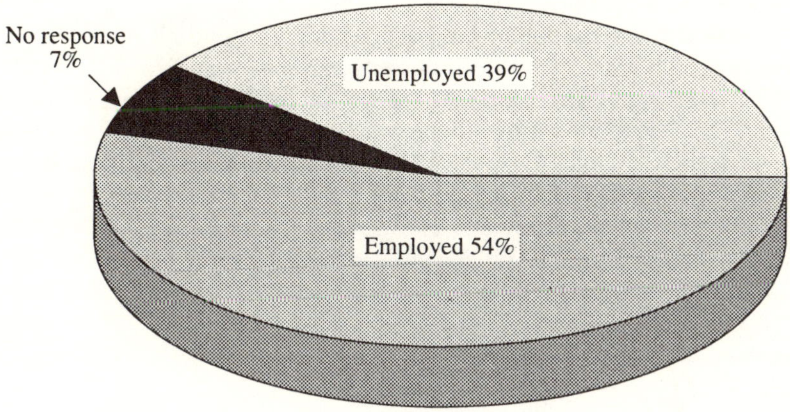

Thirty-nine percent of the sample responded that they were looking for work prior to working at an ESF-funded project, 54 percent reported that they had a job, and 7 percent had another response (Figure 4.1). Of those who had a job before joining, 60 percent had been working in construction. Five percent were vendors and 1.4 percent were miners. The rest were spread out over various occupations. Taking into account both those who came directly from mining and those who had an intervening spell of unemployment, some ten percent of the 3,050 ESF workers in the capital cities were ex-miners. Given the size of the ESF employment program at that time and the approximately 23,000 employees[3] let go when COMIBOL, the state-owned mining company, was closed, it is clear that the ESF did not come close to absorbing all of the ex-miners. However, that was never the intention of the program.

Table 4.1 Workers' Education

	ESF Workers (percent)	*Construction Workers (percent)*
None	6.3	4.4
Basic	41.2	36.8
Intermediate	24.1	15.8
Middle	26.0	26.9
Technical	0.7	3.5
Teachers' College	0.2	0.6
University	2.0	12.0
All	100.0	100.0

Source: Newman, Jorgensen, and Pradhan, 1991.

Earnings of ESF Workers

The evidence indicated that ESF workers were on the low-skilled end of the construction market, but that they were paid according to the levels prevailing in the labor market in construction. Mean monthly earnings were 225 bolivianos[4] per month for workers in ESF projects, 375 per month for the average prime-age male construction worker in the EPH sample, and 348 for the average prime-age male in the population at large. However, mean monthly earnings of low skilled construction workers in the EPH sample (those with the characteristics of ESF workers) were 196 bolivianos per month. The median of monthly earnings was 194 for workers in the ESF projects, 220 for prime-age males in the construction sector, and 230 bolivianos per month for workers in the population in general.

Hours Worked and Hourly Wages

On average, workers in ESF projects worked more hours than the prime-age males in the EPH sample. ESF workers worked 50.3 hours a week compared with 46.8 for the EPH workers. Compared with other prime-age males in the construction sector and the population in general, the distribution of hours worked by ESF workers was less variable. The mean hourly wage of workers in ESF projects was 1.16 bolivianos compared with a mean hourly wage 2.28 of the corresponding group in the EPH sample. The median hourly wage was 0.98 bolivianos for ESF workers and 1.29 bolivianos in the EPH sample.

Position of the Family

Figure 4.2 presents the distribution of the households of ESF workers across family earnings quartiles and food expenditure quartiles. Quartiles are calculated using all the families in the EPH sample. In general, ESF families appeared to be worse off if judged by per capita food expenditure quartiles rather than by family earnings quartiles. For example, 35 percent of the families were in the lowest per capita food expenditure quartile, whereas only 22 percent of the families were in the lowest family earnings quartile. This most likely reflects the fact that the jobs in the ESF were temporary. The ESF families may not have changed their expenditure patterns in response to the temporary gain in income.

The Counterfactual Simulation—The Impact of the ESF Program

Impact on ESF Workers

To ascertain the effect of the ESF, a counterfactual question was asked: what would have been the position of ESF workers and other individuals in the absence of the program? To calculate the mean benefit from working in the ESF, a calculation was made of the difference between expected wages in the ESF and the expected wages of the individuals in the absence of the ESF. This provided a picture not only of the average benefit over all ESF workers, but also of the distribution of the benefits.

In order to measure the impact of the ESF on ESF workers a three step procedure was used:[5] First, using the sample of ESF workers, an earnings function was estimated, which gave expected wages and hours worked as a function of the ESF workers' age, experience, schooling and other characteristics. This step predicts what ESF workers will earn working for the ESF.[6] The expected outcome of ESF workers working in the ESF is shown in the left half of Table 4.2.

Figure 4.2 Earnings and Food Expenditures in ESF Households

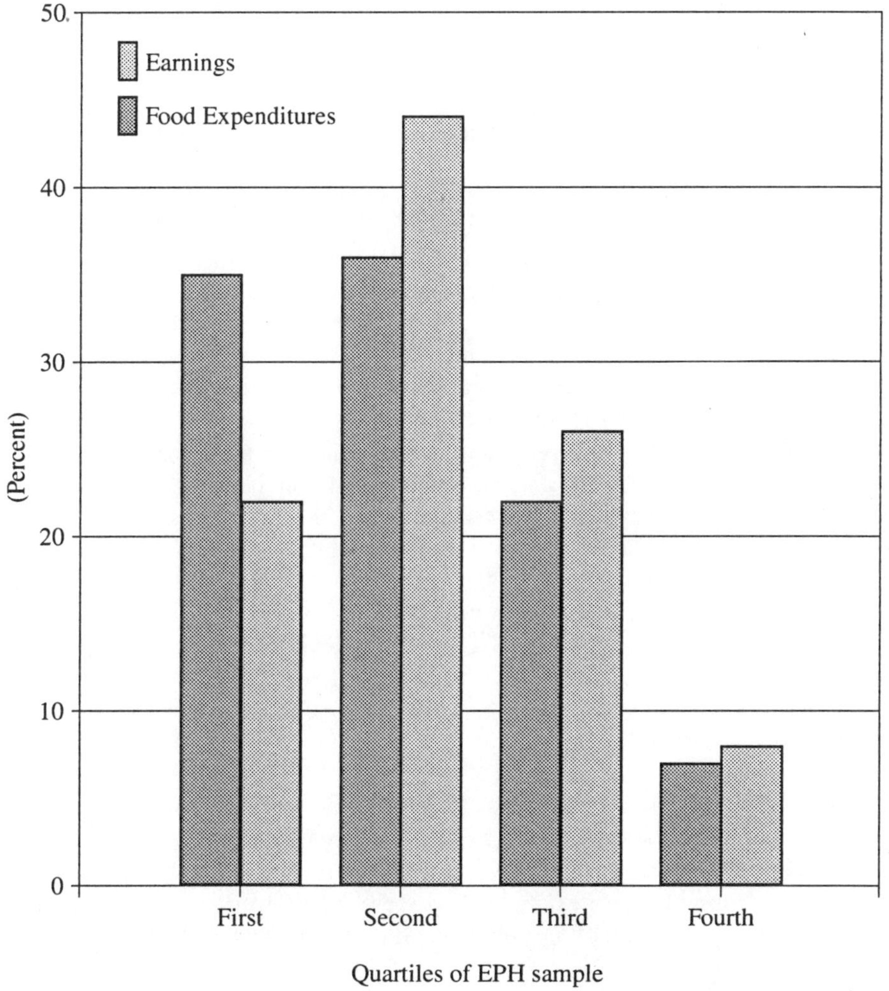

Table 4.2 Expected Position of ESF Workers

	Conditional on Working		*Unconditional*
	With ESF	*Without ESF*	*Without ESF*
Wages (bolivianos)[a]	1.15	0.94	
Weekly Hours	50.2	40.1	34.1
Weekly Earnings	57.7	38.7	34.6
Probability of Working	100%	82%	

a. At survey date, one boliviano was worth approximately $0.50.
Source: Newman, Jorgensen, and Pradhan, 1991.

Second, using the sample of prime age males in the general population, a similar earnings function and a probability of working function were estimated. Both the earnings and the probability of working were estimated as a function of the non-ESF workers' age, experience, schooling and other characteristics. This tells how experience, schooling, etc. are valued in the general labor market.

Third, the ESF workers' characteristics are plugged into the model used in the second step. This shows how the ESF workers would have fared had they been in the general labor market. This counterfactual outcome can then be compared to that of the first step. The expected outcomes for ESF workers had they worked not for the ESF, but rather worked in the general labor market, is shown in the upper half of the middle column in Table 4.2. They are outcomes conditional on working. The mean estimated probability that the ESF workers would indeed have worked, if not for the ESF, is 82 percent. Multiplying this probability by the conditional outcomes gives the unconditional outcomes, i.e., the average outcome, factoring in the probability of unemployment.

In the absence of the ESF program, its beneficiaries who found work would have been expected to receive a mean wage of 0.94 bolivianos, work an average of 40.1 hours per week and have weekly earnings of 38.7 bolivianos per week. The mean probability that the ESF workers would have been working in the absence of the program was 82 percent. Thus, their mean unconditional weekly hours worked were 34.1 hours with mean weekly earnings of 34.6 bolivianos.

Over the whole ESF sample, the average ESF worker experienced a 22 percent increase in wages, an increase of 10.1 hours of work a week, and a 45 percent increase in weekly earnings over what he would have earned if he had been working in the absence of the ESF. Taking into account the probability that the individual may not have worked in the absence of the ESF leads to larger gains. The unconditional comparison indicated that the average ESF worker received an increase of 16.1 hours of work a week, and a 67 percent increase in earnings.

Comparing the effects on various income groups gives a result as shown in Figure 4.3. This shows that, for example, 25 percent of ESF workers would have belonged to the poorest tenth of the population had they not had the ESF work. With

Figure 4.3 Distribution of ESF Workers by EPH Decile

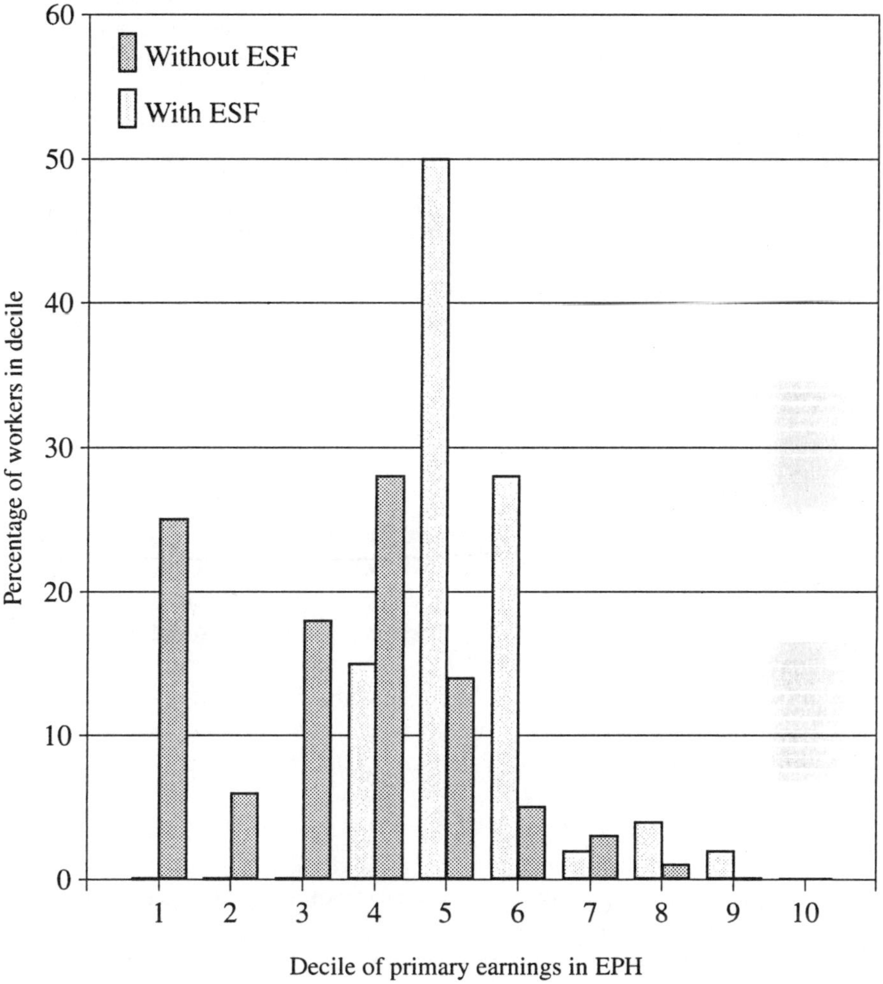

the ESF job, none belonged to the poorest group. The effect of the ESF job was to concentrate the workers in the middle of the income distribution. This would indicate that the poorest have obtained the largest absolute benefit, a hypothesis confirmed by the data.

Impact on the Labor Market in General

In principle, the effect of the ESF on the labor market positions could be estimated by holding constant for local labor market conditions and estimating the incremental effect of the ESF on wage offers. As the ESF increased the demand for labor, one would have expected to see the ESF have a positive effect on wage offers and, therefore, lead to increases in the probability of working and in hours worked. To infer the position of non-ESF workers in the absence of the ESF, one would have included a measure of ESF activity among the determinants of wages and hours worked. The difference between the predicted wages with the ESF variable and without it would have shown the incremental effect of the ESF program.

Several measures of the size of the ESF program were used without success. It proved impossible to measure any spill-over benefits of the ESF program on other workers who did not participate in the program. However, given that the total amount of ESF workers employed in capital cities at the time of the survey amounted to just 0.3 percent of the economically active population and 2.7 percent of the total number of unemployed, any spill-over effects would have been expected to be minimal.

Conclusions

Based on the simulations, the ESF generated substantial temporary gains in earnings of workers at ESF-funded projects, over what they would have received in the absence of the program. The lowest income groups received the greatest increases in earnings. While most of the workers still received low incomes even with the program, there was some leakage in that some individuals in the higher earnings deciles did benefit from the ESF. The ESF did not target the ex-employees of the public sector who are generally considered to have been the persons most directly affected by Bolivia's structural adjustment program. The ESF did employ workers that came from the construction industry, which was hurt by the economic crisis which preceded and prompted the adjustment program.

The subcontractors could hire whoever they thought could do the work. No specific requirements to hire miners, women, or workers of any particular background were imposed. Thus the workers hired were very similar to those in the general construction sector. Temporary employment schemes in other countries have sought to improve targeting of wage benefits by imposing restrictions or quotas on who may be hired. In general this is difficult to do when working through contractors, as enforcement is costly and uncertain. Furthermore, if the workers who are sought are not those who normally work in construction related activities, the quality of work may be lower and/or supervision costs higher than if no hiring restrictions are imposed.

Other temporary employment schemes have opted for requiring below market wages. In the ESF the underlying market philosophy of the adjustment program ran strong. As with quotas, below market wages would also tend to increase concerns about the quality of work. The fact that so few ex-miners worked on ESF jobs indicates that either they chose not to apply, having found better employment or they were regarded as inferior workers by the contractors.

The implication for other countries considering an ESF is that if the infrastructure built (the output of the employment/income maintenance program) is valued highly, then it may still be considered desirable to use a market-based hiring system even though the mix of the workers hired may not match the desired targets. The ESF's low-cost administrative procedures and extensive management controls, together with its use of private subcontractors, enabled it to rapidly generate temporary benefits for workers who came mainly from low income groups. If this outcome is considered acceptable, then this type of temporary employment scheme may be a viable alternative to programs where the government directly hires workers.

Notes

1. This chapter is a condensed and simplified version of the authors' article in the *World Bank Economic Review* (1991).
2. At the time of INE's Survey (May 1988), the size of the ESF program was still picking up speed and small relative to the labor force. In all ESF-sponsored economic infrastructure projects in the capital cities, 3,051 persons were employed. This number constituted 0.3 percent of the economically active population and 2.7 percent of the unemployed in the capital cities.
3. About two-thirds of whom were administrators.
4. At the time of the survey, one boliviano was worth about $0.50.
5. The full econometric model and more detailed results are presented in Newman, Jorgensen and Pradhan, 1991.
6. Model predictions, rather than the actual outcome in the ESF, were used in the comparison because the outcomes in the ESF may reflect characteristics not measured in the data and would therefore give a biased comparison with the scenario in the absence of the ESF.

5

Procurement Heresy at the ESF

by Graham Smith

The Bolivian Emergency Social Fund's (ESF's) procurement procedures were unconventional, simple and efficient. They were entirely in character with the ESF's "emergency" orientation, and with its desire to extract the maximum possible benefit from every dollar of funding received.

Procurement Orthodoxy

In terms of the conventional wisdom governing public procurement, the ESF's practices—particularly its direct dealings with contractors chosen freely by project sponsors—amounted to heresy in the extreme. Procurement policy and practice at the World Bank dictate that contracts should be awarded through a process of open bidding. At least three sorts of arguments are traditionally offered in favor of open bidding. First, competition will ensure that the right prices are paid: contractors know that if they bid too high they won't get the job, and if they bid too low, they won't make a profit. Second, contractors know best how to estimate the costs of a job. They know what local labor and materials cost, what the productivity of their labor is, and what combination of labor and machinery is best suited to local conditions and relative prices. No central agency, such as the ESF, can have as thorough an understanding of all the ins and outs as the contractor himself. Third, the discretionary element in the choosing of a contractor should be kept to a minimum. Selection should be based on a uniform set of rules, applied without discrimination, so that no one is open to bribery.

The ESF's Heresy

ESF Procurement Procedures

Contractors' Selection. The vast majority of ESF infrastructure projects were, in a nutshell, contracted in the following manner: once a project received approval from the ESF's board of directors, it became the responsibility of the local organization that had sponsored the project to nominate a contractor. The ESF exercised no influence over the choice of contractor: it gave no guidelines to the sponsoring groups, nor did it require them to choose a contractor through open bidding. The contractor chosen by the sponsor received from the ESF a take-it-or-leave-it financial offer for taking on the project. The non-negotiable price set by the ESF was based on its unit cost system.

ESF's Unit Cost. The heart of the procurement procedure followed by the ESF was its unit cost system, which it applied to most infrastructure projects. The ESF developed a schedule of standard prices for the completion of various types of projects. In the case of an urban street-paving project, the ESF would offer the contractor a set amount per square meter of street; for a housing project, so much per house, and for a sewerage project, so much per meter of pipe laid. On top of the basic amount determined by the unit costs, the ESF would allow the contractor an additional 10 percent for overhead, and 5 percent for profit, margins considerably lower than contractors in Bolivia normally built into tenders submitted for competitive bids.

The essential point here was that the ESF operated on the principle of paying not for the contractor's inputs (labor and material), but rather for the *results* of the work. The standard costs schedule was continually revised, and also incorporated, to the greatest extent feasible, regional variations in prices.

The ESF's Procurement Rationale

The ESF felt that the standard arguments about procurement were inappropriate, both in view of its mandate and of local conditions in Bolivia. It advanced four counter-arguments in response to the Bank's concerns:

First, in the case of the kinds of works contemplated in Bolivia, the ESF did in fact have a better idea than the contractors themselves of the costs involved. ESF infrastructure projects tended to be quite small, worth $60,000 to $70,000 on average. Small-scale undertakings such as these would not typically be carried out by large, highly organized contractors, but rather by what were essentially "one-man" operations, employing perhaps a dozen workers and owning a small amount of machinery. Such contractors would most probably not keep orderly or thorough accounts, would not be able to estimate, ahead of time, the productivity of their workforce, would not always know where to buy materials at the best price, and would not know, when making a bid, what sorts of payoffs they might have to make down the line. These contractors were, in sum, ill-informed and risk-averse, and would therefore be expected to bid up the price of a job to a level higher than what the ESF believed was reasonable to cover materials and overhead and allow for a normal profit.

Second, bidders in Bolivia collude. They operate in a thin market, where many of the players are personally acquainted. When a call for bids goes out, it is routine for contractors to get together and agree on "who should get this one."

Third, although project sponsors were given virtually complete discretion in choosing a contractor, the nature of the standard price system meant that potential contractors would have little incentive to bribe sponsoring agencies. The standard prices, with their moderate margins for overhead and profit, were "fat-free"; paying a bribe of any substance would probably make the project an uneconomic proposition for the contractor.

Fourth, the ESF was intensely concerned about the speed of its operations. It was aiming to approve projects at a rate of up to 20 per week. But the standard public sector competitive bidding procedure was fraught with delays and inefficiency. Losing bidders, for example, could be expected as a matter of course to file appeals, tying the process up for weeks or months. Having to adhere to this process would block the ESF from achieving its targeted volume of contracting, seriously compromising its role as an "emergency" organization charged with doing as much as possible, as quickly as possible, to alleviate the social costs of the country's economic crisis.

Rules and Safeguards

Bidding for Large Contracts. The agreement arrived at with the World Bank stipulated that the ESF could use its standard price system for contracts valued at up to $250,000. As it happened, this ceiling covered 85 percent to 90 percent of contracts awarded by the ESF. Contracts above this threshold (up to $750,000, the maximum the Bolivian government allowed the ESF to grant to any one project) had to be put out to tender. But even in the latter cases, the ESF sought informally to impose the discipline of its standard pricing system. If all bids on a project came in above the standard price, the ESF would often negotiate with the lowest bidder to bring him down to the indicated price.[1]

Total Award Limits. Because the ESF's procurement procedures were so unusual, and, at least in principle, prone to corruption, the Bank insisted on a series of safeguards. The Bank was particularly concerned about the virtually complete freedom given to project sponsors to select contractors, a state of affairs that might easily lead sponsors to seek payoffs for awarding contracts, or, alternatively, induce contractors to offer bribes. Accordingly, the Bank required that no one contractor be allowed, over the life of the ESF, to receive more than $500,000 of contracts, except in cases where the contractor had won the jobs by competitive bidding, or in cases where no other contractors had come forward. With the ESF nearly complete at the time of this writing, the record shows that indeed few contractors have won more than $500,000 of business from the ESF. However, it now appears that some contractors may have exceeded the limit by registering their companies under different names.

Audit of Unit Costs. The Bank also asked the ESF to hire a technical auditor who would ascertain that the standard unit costs continued to be set at reasonable levels. A comparison of ESF prices with prices paid by the municipality of La Paz for similar works contracted under competitive bidding found the ESF's prices to be typically 20 percent to 30 percent lower.

Performance Bond. The ESF required all contractors to post a performance bond worth 20 percent of the project cost. If problems arose (funds were misused, projects were not completed, or were of inadequate quality), the ESF could cash in the bond and use the proceeds to set things to rights. Since the ESF only gave advances in the amount of 20 percent, it was covered against most potential losses.

Procurement Reviews. Finally, the Bank itself undertook to do quarterly reviews of procurement. Prepared by a consultant based at the Bank's resident mission in La Paz, the reports focused on three key indicators: change orders, delays in implementation, and quality problems.

Change Orders. In some cases, additions to the contract to cover extra work ("change orders") were agreed to by the ESF after the contract had been signed. A large number of change orders, or an unexpected pattern in their occurrence, could conceivably be a sign of collusion between contractors and regionally-based ESF "zone chiefs." Consider, for example, a case where the ESF agreed to fund one kilometer of urban street paving. Assume that the contractor could complete an additional quarter kilometer of paving at no additional fixed cost. The contractor might be tempted to bribe the zone chief to recommend that an additional quarter-kilometer of paving be done. With the ESF's grant covering his variable costs, and with his fixed costs already covered by the amount awarded under the original contract, the 10 percent margin allowed by the ESF for overhead would, in the case of the additional work, amount to a windfall profit.

The quarterly procurement reviews found no evidence of systematic problems related to change orders. They occurred in about 25 percent of all contracts, but the magnitude of the changes amounted to only 2-3 percent of the cost of the portfolio. The main cause was poor technical design that required adjustments during project execution.

Delays in Implementation. The procurement reviews did find that substantial time overruns were more the rule than the exception. It was not unusual for projects to require 150 percent, or more, of the budgeted time for completion. Interpreting this phenomenon was no simple matter. It may have been a sign that the unit costs were too low, leading contractors to string out projects while they sought to cross-subsidize them with income from other jobs. Or, it may simply have been a consequence of inexperience, both on the part of contractors who may not have fully understood the magnitude of the projects they agreed to undertake, and of ESF staff, who (like many World Bank task managers) tended to be chronically over-optimistic in estimating the time it would take to implement projects.

Quality Problems. Sub-standard quality of works was one of the most serious start-up problems that the ESF had to grapple with (see Chapter 2). One obvious explanation would be that the unit costs were too low, leading contractors to scrimp on workmanship and use poor quality materials. But actual experience and anecdotal evidence suggest that the quality problems were more likely attributable to inexperience on the part of contractors, supervising agencies and the ESF staff alike.

Blacklisting. One interesting safeguard that the ESF itself developed was an informal "blacklist" of contractors. The list contained the names of contractors who were disqualified from receiving more ESF work because of what had been deemed extremely unsatisfactory performance on previous contracts. This was intended, again, as a counterbalance against the wide degree of freedom given to project sponsors to choose contractors. This practice of course deviated substantially from the World Bank's standard procurement practices. Under the latter rules, the only way a contractor may be disqualified from taking on a contract would be if the contractor failed to meet formal prequalification standards. These standards would be applied universally—i.e., they could not simply be used to block out a particular contractor—and would focus on factors such as a potential contractor's financial health, technical capability, past performance in similar work, and so forth.

The ESF's informal blacklist was, like the rest of its unconventional procurement regime, well suited to local conditions and practices. Disqualification procedures would probably have been difficult to make formal for the kinds of small contractors involved, given that their activities are not highly formalized, business and personal relationships tend to overlap more often than not, and people will generally avoid making written complaints about unsatisfactory performance. Obviously, an informal blacklisting procedure may easily be corrupted. It was a tribute to the quality of the ESF's management team that theirs was not.

Conclusions

Did the ESF pay contractors too much? There are no conclusive data upon which one might draw to determine, definitively, whether or not the ESF's unit costs were set too high. The limited evidence available suggests, however, that if anything, the ESF's pricing came out on the low side. The above-noted comparison of ESF contracts with contracts awarded under competitive bidding by the municipality of La Paz was one indication; it was also observed that in the relatively small number of cases where the ESF put contracts out to tender, even the lowest bids tended to come in at a price higher than what would have been prescribed by the ESF's cost schedule.

Measured by the goals the ESF set for itself—to contract out small-scale public works projects quickly, simply, honestly and at the right prices—the unit cost scheme proved to be a highly successful experiment. There is no obvious reason for other countries planning to inaugurate similar funds not to consider adopting the same sort of process, all the standard arguments in favor of competitive bidding notwithstanding.

Certain conditions must, of course, apply if this type of procurement is to work well. The large amount of discretion built into the ESF's scheme was balanced by a system of close monitoring and safeguards. Rigorous accountability mechanisms—the ESF routinely submitted reports on its spending to the Bolivian Congress and the press—were also important.

Equally, if not more, important, but considerably less tangible a factor, was the quality of the ESF's staff. From the outset, the ESF was blessed with a committed staff that worked to the highest standards of professionalism and integrity. No amount of effort to create provisions for monitoring and accountability could have kept the procurement system as honest as it was if the persons involved in its day-to-day operation had been determined to corrupt it.

Notes

1. This practice of entering into negotiations following the completion of a tender was also stretching the World Bank's rules, which permit such negotiations only when the lowest bid exceeds the contracting party's estimate by a large margin.

6

Working with Non-governmental Organizations

by Julie VanDomelen

With the creation of the Emergency Social Fund (ESF), the government of Bolivia entered into its first experience in financing projects executed by agencies outside of the public sector. Non-governmental organizations (NGOs) were included in the list of agencies eligible to present project proposals to the ESF. Due to the high level of funding that went to NGOs and the broad range of organizations and types of projects receiving ESF support, this experiment served to highlight both the risks and advantages of a more direct relation between NGOs and the public sector. This chapter explores the experience of the ESF in working with NGOs and draws some general conclusions that may be useful beyond the Bolivian context.

Background

Profile of NGOs in Bolivia

Because of the heterogeneity of NGOs in Bolivia, it is useful to classify these organizations into four main types: religious organizations, local NGOs, internationally based private voluntary organizations (PVOs), and grassroots organizations ("organisaciones de base"). Each type of organization tends to differ in its objectives, methods of operation, and organizational structure. This chapter will mainly use the term "NGO" in the generic sense, but will distinguish between types of NGOs where necessary (e.g., when referring to ESF data bases).

Among NGOs, religious organizations have been active in Bolivia for the longest period of time. Due to the nature of these organizations, they have extensive national coverage and have accumulated a large infrastructure in health and education. The Catholic Church accounts for 18 percent of formal education coverage in the country. With a commitment to serving the poor, religious organizations have taken a central role in programs to provide assistance to both the structurally poor and the most vulnerable groups affected by the economic adjustment process.

Local NGOs are extremely varied. Most operate relatively small projects in integrated rural development with an emphasis on community education and participation. These actions are typically centered on a specific geographical area or community. With a shift in interest of external donors, local NGOs have multiplied rapidly in the last ten years. It is estimated that approximately 600 local NGOs exist, with the majority having been in operation for less than ten years. Many have a political or ideological edge honed during the years of dictatorship in Bolivia. While the return to democracy has eased some of the tension between the government and these NGOs, a tradition of mistrust and political opposition had caused these organizations to view with skepticism the possibility of working with the ESF.

The international PVOs focus their activities in a number of clearly delimited geographical areas, and generally seek to provide integrated basic services, including health care, education, water supply and sanitation, and agricultural development. The approach is technocratic compared with religious organizations and local NGOs. With their range of actions determined by their relationship with external funding sources, the idea of being assisted by a Bolivian agency like the ESF was novel.

Grassroots organizations differ from the previous types of NGOs in that they are composed of the beneficiaries themselves, rather than serving as intermediaries. Grassroots organizations are spontaneously formed in response to specific local needs or common interests. Such groups include mothers' clubs, local water agencies, cooperatives, neighborhood councils, miners' wives organizations, and so on. While representing beneficiary interests more directly and legitimately than many other types of NGOs, these organizations are often characterized by weak and fluctuating individual leadership that often speaks for only one of a competing set of local interests. The major concern of the ESF in financing projects presented by these organizations was that they would not have the sufficient technical or administrative capacity to execute projects efficiently.

The Context for NGO-Government Collaboration

The ESF faced numerous obstacles in establishing working relationships with NGOs. There existed little trust and no established mechanisms for bringing these very distinct types of agencies into a collaborative relationship with the government. Based on ideological grounds or concern over the social impact of adjustment, many NGOs voiced strong opposition to the adjustment program, of which the ESF was an integral part. At the time many were questioning not only the adjustment measures, but broader economic issues such as the debt burden and which segments of Bolivian society would be forced to pay this debt. This resulted in additional opposition to the source of ESF financing, particularly credit from such institutions as the World Bank. This environment of polarization, severe social emergency, and economic adjustment was not the most likely backdrop for new initiatives in forming a more creative relationship between the government and NGOs.

Despite the rather unpromising economic and institutional environment, the decision was made on the part of the government to include NGOs in the ESF program. This was largely due to a consideration of very immediate macroeconomic imperatives, rather than a more circumspect policy vision of how the public and NGO sectors could cooperate. The ESF needed to channel money quickly and efficiently to create temporary employment and social services. Line ministries were considered incapable of offering the speed and project-driven approach necessary. NGOs were already recognized as playing an important role in the delivery of social assistance. To stabilize the provision of these services, NGOs were therefore sought out specifically to present assistance projects to the ESF including nutrition programs, informal technical training and delivery of health services.

Obstacles and Mechanisms to Overcome Them

Reluctance to Work with the Government

Mechanisms had to be developed within the ESF to overcome four primary obstacles that threatened to impede working with NGOs. There was a deep-seated reluctance on the part of NGOs—based on mistrust—to enter into a relationship with the government. Several policies were adopted and actions taken to alleviate this tension.[1] The ESF adopted a policy of non-interference in the internal affairs and overall financial resources of NGOs. Historically, when the government has sought any kind of coordination with NGOs on a global level, these overtures have been accompanied by policies designed to control the NGOs and their use of external resources, so the ESF's approach was novel. The ESF's method of operating with efficiency and transparency persuaded the NGOs that the government was serious in its intentions and would comply with its commitments in a strictly professional manner. A further factor that should not be underestimated was the hiring policies of the ESF. By recruiting a technical staff of dynamic, committed and politically diverse people, several of whom had been involved with NGOs, confidence was won on a personal level (more so than on an institutional level) that the ESF would deal fairly with NGOs.

In addition to these general policy measures, some concrete actions were taken to invite full NGO access to the ESF. An active promotion strategy was used to start a dialogue with NGOs to inform them of the opportunities available through the ESF and of procedures that needed to be followed in presenting projects. When this initial information campaign met with continued skepticism, ESF staff sought to create a demonstration effect by offering financing to a few well-established and respected NGOs, the most important of which was the health-related San Gabriel Foundation. By demonstrating how the ESF would operate with NGOs, a foundation of legitimacy was established.

Number and Diversity of NGOs

The second potential obstacle to channeling money through NGOs was the perceived difficulty of organizing a more intensive relationship with NGOs in the face of their sheer number and diversity. In the search for a greater response in social assistance projects, the ESF created a mechanism which attempted to work through an association of NGOs. In March 1989, the ESF signed a contract with a national network of NGOs that work in the health sector. This network, FENASONGS, was a relatively new effort at coordination between NGOs. While the experience of FENASONGS with the ESF was very difficult for both parties, it does point to some of the advantages and pitfalls of working through networks.

The basics of the agreement were as follows: FENASONGS promised to present 80 health projects to the ESF on behalf of its member (and non-member) organizations within 12 months of the signing of the agreement and the ESF, in turn, agreed to earmark funds to finance those projects. In addition, the ESF agreed to finance a technical staff through FENASONGS to assist member and non-member NGOs in the preparation and presentation of health projects to the ESF. This technical team was also to supervise the projects, receiving 2.5 percent of the dollar value of each project supervised. While very solid conceptually, this agreement broke down due to a variety of factors.

FENASONGS was unable to deliver the 80 projects promised due to a miscalculation of demand from potential beneficiaries and a realization that the way most NGOs works required a fairly long start-up period to facilitate community participation. In addition, projects were presented that NGOs considered within the health sector (e.g., potable water and sewerage), but which the ESF did not include within its own definition of "health" projects, (The ESF, while not disputing what was or was not health, was seeking to meet programming targets for projects defined in standard ways). One of the most contentious issues was whether FENASONGS projects should receive special treatment. Several were rejected by the ESF on technical grounds; FENASONGS reacted by accusing the ESF of acting in bad faith. In addition, several FENASONGS member NGOs had health projects approved and financed very quickly without having to go through FENASONGS, making FENASONGS a less important interlocutor in the eyes of member NGOs.

The experience with FENASONGS raised a basic issue about working with NGO networks in the context of the ESF. Most NGO networks in Bolivia serve to formulate coherent policies between NGOs, exchange information, and create a united front in negotiations with the government. In Bolivia, these networks were in the formative stages, and had difficulty defining a common voice that represents all members. The agreement between the ESF and FENASONGS required that FENASONGS get involved at a technical level with its member organizations, and that it exercise some authority (i.e., supervision and control) over its members. Neither of these requirements played to FENASONGS's comparative advantage, which was in the areas of negotiating on behalf of NGOs and sharing information between NGOs.

Rivalry for Resources

The third obstacle to ESF-NGO collaboration was the potential rivalry between public agencies and NGOs for ESF resources. At a time of falling government revenues and stretched line agency budgets, it could be expected that channelling resources through NGOs, which were already viewed with jealousy due to their access to foreign financing, would be treated with resistance by other public agencies. The ESF decided to adopt a very neutral policy; all types of organizations were equally eligible for ESF financing and projects were reviewed on a purely technical basis. ESF's objectives were not to be met through *whom* they funded, but *what* they funded. This policy effectively silenced any serious opposition from the line ministries who, rather than focus their attention on controlling NGO finances, were putting their technical staffs to work elaborating projects of their own for the ESF. In fact, as a group, public agencies received the bulk of ESF financing, which served to distract attention from the flow through NGOs. The rules of the game created a healthy atmosphere of competition among agencies, both public and private, to present technically sound projects to the ESF.

Questionable Institutional Capacity

The fourth obstacle that faced the ESF was a doubt about the capability of the smaller NGOs, especially grassroots organizations, to design and execute projects effectively. While NGOs had a reputation for being more effective and inventive than state agencies, their implementation capacity was relatively untested. The pool of NGOs contained a mix of institutions with differences in administrative capacity and a lack of common criteria and systems. In response to this situation, the ESF's promotion department (see Chapter 3) took two actions. First, institutional support projects were designed to strengthen directly some of the key NGOs working with the ESF, such as CARITAS. These projects contained financing to hire short-term technical personnel and pay selected operational expenditures related to elaborating and executing ESF projects. Second, promotion staff lent technical support in the filling out of project profiles presented by weaker religious and grassroots organizations.

A further factor that helped shore up weak institutional capacity was the very way in which the ESF operated. Its attention to financing specific projects with itemized budgets, strict cost control, use of private contractors and an intensive system of site visits during project implementation lent itself to easier execution by weaker agencies. Within these parameters, the implementing capacity of grassroots organizations was often cited as being equal to that of more technically proficient public agencies. However, the distinction between financing programs and projects was important. ESF staff noted the relative deficiencies of many of the weaker NGOs to plan long range strategies and coherent programs. In the case of specific projects, however, execution was manageable. Going the next step to financing NGO interventions on a program basis could be (quite) risky.

The Outcome: Profile of ESF Financing through NGOs

Non-governmental organizations accounted for one-quarter of the value of projects approved by the ESF, or $43.8 million, as of June 18, 1990. NGO-sponsored projects representing thirty percent of the total number of approved projects. Table 6.1 presents a sectorial distribution of projects by type of requesting agency.

In social assistance, local NGOs, international PVOs and religious organizations accounted for over half of ESF projects. The category "Other Ministries" includes the Ministry of Health, which represented the only other significant organizational presence in social assistance projects. The Ministry of Health participated largely through a limited number of large projects in vaccinations and epidemic control. The large share from religious organizations and NGOs highlights the importance these organizations had in the institutional setting of Bolivia for providing nutrition and health services and training.

In social infrastructure, public agencies have accounted for the lion's share of ESF projects. This was largely due to the specialized central agencies like the National Council for School Construction (CONES) in school construction and the Ministry of Urban Affairs in the housing sector. The significant presence of the regional development corporations was concentrated primarily in projects for water supply and sewerage. While social infrastructure projects were viewed by NGOs as an important component of their programs (see Table 6.2), NGOs tended to cover more limited geographical areas and often lacked the technical capacity and mandate to design and carry out larger-scale projects.

As would be expected, municipalities, the National Road Service, and the regional development corporations accounted for the bulk of economic infrastructure projects. These projects included urban improvements, road maintenance, erosion control, drainage and irrigation. While all types of NGOs received funding for economic infrastructure projects, again, the projects tended to be smaller in scale, with the exception of larger food-for-work projects in urban upgrading run through two major religious organizations.

Following a natural division of labor, cooperatives had the largest share of what the ESF defined as "productive" projects. These projects were divided into revolving credit funds and, in more exceptional cases, the production of materials like sewer pipes to be used in larger scale civil works projects financed by the ESF. Regional development corporations and municipalities were involved only in the production of materials, while revolving funds represented the more conventional idea of a sustainable, productive project. In this area, cooperatives, NGOs, reli-

Table 6.1 Distribution of ESF Projects by Requesting Agency as of June 18, 1990 (percent)

	Total	*Social Assistance*	*Social Infrastructure*	*Economic Infrastructure*	*Productive Projects*	*Institutional Support*
NGOs	7	21	5	5	14	8
Religious Organizations	9	30	8	5	5	28
Grassroots Organizations	6	6	7	5	7	–
Cooperatives	3	1	2	1	26	12
Subtotal	25	57	21	16	52	48
Municipalities	17	2	9	30	10	2
Regional Dev. Corps.	16	1	15	20	7	–
National Road Service	8	–	–	19	5	–
CONES[a]	4	7	7	–	–	–
Other Ministries	12	19	19	3	–	2
Prefectures	5	8	5	5	–	–
JNSDS[b]	2	–	4	–	–	2
Others	13	6	18	7	25	47
Total	100	100	100	100	100	100

a. National Council for School Construction
b. National Association for Solidarity and Social Development
Source: ESF.

gious organizations and grassroots organizations together represented 99 percent of total ESF financing.

The final project category, institutional support, reflected the ESF's decisions about which institutions, of those seeking ESF funding for projects, could and should receive additional support. If the original concept of institutional support projects was to facilitate better project preparation and supervision, it is then interesting to look at the ratio between the amount spent on institutional support and the dollar value of projects implemented by those institutions. Nine types of organizations received institutional support. Of the more significant recipients, the most intensive support went to the category "other government entities" that received on average, about $0.10 for every dollar granted for project implementation. Cooperatives were next $0.04 per dollar, religious organizations received $0.03 per dollar, and local NGOs and international PVOs $0.01.[2] One notable gap was the absence of institutional support programs for grassroots organizations. The difficulty here was lack of a mechanism, not lack of need. The ESF tended to concentrate support on larger organizations that were presenting packets of projects. This is understandable and probably an optimal use of resources, but it meant that the ESF could not reach the universe of small, dispersed and unorganized grassroots organizations upon which, in the end, the ESF relied for a healthy portion of its portfolio.

While Table 6.1 showed the importance of various types of institutions to the ESF, Table 6.2 reveals the priorities that the various types of NGOs had in presenting projects to the ESF. While the ESF relied heavily on NGOs for social assistance and productive projects as shown in Table 6.1, the NGOs came to the ESF primarily for infrastructure, both social and economic, as shown in Table 6.2. The one exception to this is the specialization of cooperatives on productive projects, which accounted for a large part of their demand.

Given their strong development mandate, local NGOs and PVOs might be expected to present the strongest demand from the ESF. However, Table 6.2 shows that, in fact, religious organizations received the largest share of financing. Also, grassroots organizations received $10.4 million in ESF financing, far surpassing expectations of the capacity of these organizations as a channel for development financing.

The statistics show that NGOs as a whole served as an important outlet for ESF financing, and were vital to carrying out the ESF's program in certain sectors. While NGOs tend to put more emphasis on presenting certain types of projects, they have outperformed other types of organizations in terms of reaching across sectors. Indeed of the 22 categories of ESF projects, only religious organizations had projects in all. Grassroots organizations represented all but one; and NGOs all but two. Public agencies tend to show a greater degree of specialization.

Issues

Poverty Targeting of NGOs

Given the NGOs' reputation for concentrating their interventions on the poorer segments of Bolivian society, the ESF hoped that including them as requesting agencies would help to target resources to the neediest beneficiaries. While the poverty level of beneficiary communities had not been determined, existing poverty maps provided a proxy by dividing Bolivia's 99 provinces into poverty rankings of 1 through 5, with 5 denoting provinces of the most critical poverty.

Table 6.2 Distribution of ESF Projects to NGOs as of June 18, 1990 (percent)

	Local NGOs and PVOs	*Religious Organizations*	*Grassroots Organizations*	*Cooperatives*
Social Assistance	27	29	8	2
Economic Infrastructure	29	23	34	17
Social Infrastructure	35	43	53	40
Productive Activities	8	2	5	37
Institutional Support	1	3	—	4
Total	100	100	100	100
Total ESF Financing	12.2	16.4	10.4	4.8

Source: ESF.

Table 6.3 presents a distribution of the demand for ESF financing by province, poverty levels and requesting agencies. The figure for demand is used instead of project approvals because it better represents the underlying tendency of the type of requesting agencies to work in selected areas.

Summing the percentage of requests coming from poverty areas 4 and 5 as indicative of the poorest, largely rural, provinces, the strongest relative demand came from the National Road Service which can be explained by its focus on road construction and upgrading outside of urban areas. NGOs show a stronger inclination to cover poor, rural areas than do religious and grassroots organizations; however, this finding may be skewed by the presence of large, urban-based food-for-work projects run by religious organizations. The general rule of thumb in Bolivia was that in the most isolated and poorest rural provinces, the church was typically the only organized institutional presence. NGOs, religious organizations and grassroots organizations all have stronger demand coming from poorer areas than do the centralized public agencies like CONES and the Ministry of Health. In this respect NGO participation in the ESF did help to target resources to the poor. However, it should be noted that none of these organizations directed the majority of its resources to the poorest, most remote regions.

Leveraging Resources through the Use of NGOs

The ESF sought to increase external flows into Bolivia, and to leverage these flows to attract additional investment from local agencies. As a rule, the ESF imposed no requirements for counterpart funding, but would attempt to secure it when circumstances permitted. Counterpart funds were also used to assure that requesting agencies had a financial stake in successful implementation. Table 6.4 reviews the experience of the ESF in securing counterpart financing from

Table 6.3 Distribution of ESF Projects by Poverty Area and Type of Requesting Agency as of March 1989 (percent of amount solicited)

Organization	*Poverty Area 1*	*Poverty Area 2*	*Poverty Area 3*	*Poverty Area 4*	*Poverty Area 5*	*Total*
NGO	28	12	22	31	7	100
Religious	48	30	9	10	4	100
Grassroots	28	28	27	12	5	100
Reg. Dev. Corps.	26	33	17	17	8	100
Natl. Road Serv.	9	21	27	34	9	100
CONES[a]	78	13	4	5	0	100
Ministry of Health	55	15	18	8	5	100
Prefectures	27	25	24	18	5	100

a. National Council for School Construction
Source: ESF.

Table 6.4 Counterpart Contributions to ESF Projects by Requesting Agency—March 1989 (percent)

Agency	*Counterpart as Share of Total Project Cost*
Religious Organizations	
Rural	6.99
Urban	20.80
Total	17.10
Grassroots Organizations/Cooperatives	
Rural	15.87
Urban	14.17
Total	15.15
Municipalities	
Rural	18.61
Urban	12.97
Total	14.65
NGOs	
Rural	13.92
Urban	3.72
Total	11.12
Regional Development Corporations	
Rural	8.67
Urban	9.30
Total	8.89
Other Government Agencies	
Rural	1.95
Urban	7.26
Total	4.75

Source: ESF.

requesting agencies. The figures include financial contributions and donations of equipment; however, they do not include estimated costs for donated labor and materials.

Surprisingly, the highest overall shares of counterpart financing for ESF projects were provided by religious organizations, cooperatives and grassroots organizations. The fact that cooperatives and grassroots organizations were able to generate close to $2.4 million was unexpected given their reputation for existing on a shoestring and having little capacity to generate significant resources. Though grassroots organizations and cooperatives do often run on very limited budgets and have little access to external resources, the fact that they were comprised of the beneficiaries themselves was shown to be an important factor in generating internal financial contributions to leverage investments.

Analyzing Implementation Capacity of NGOs

No complete evaluation exists of the quality of implementation of ESF projects, making it difficult to assess the relative implementation capacity of NGOs. The only source of reliable statistical information on implementation problems was the list of project contracts canceled by the ESF. However, contracts can be canceled for a myriad of reasons, including problems with private contractors, poor appraisal on the part of the ESF, or weaknesses within the requesting agency.

While implementation by any type of NGO was not without its problems, these problem projects represented a very small proportion of total NGO projects and their numbers were not out of line with problem projects sponsored by other types of institutions. As of June 19, 1990, six projects were listed as in the process of being canceled, and 35 had been canceled. Two of the six projects involved a religious organization implementing food-for-work construction projects. The ESF had historically had difficulties with these types of projects, which were organizationally complex, required significant counterpart funding and often employed workers who were unskilled in construction. Of the 35 canceled projects, five were presented by NGOs, two by religious organizations, three by cooperatives, and three by grassroots organizations. Technical or administrative deficiencies accounted for three of the NGO cancellations, one cooperative project and one project from a religious organization.

Based on discussions with ESF staff and numerous field visits, one can form a general outline of the implementation capacity of different types of NGOs. (All the normal caveats applied to broad generalizations of course apply here). Religious organizations tended to be the most efficient in the stretching of resources, but tended to focus on immediate relief and assistance efforts rather than long-term programs. While they could offer few concrete assurances of continuing these activities once ESF financing stopped, in the end they most often found a way. They also tended to be less ambitious than the local NGOs in the extension of their services and in expansion to other activities, probably in part because of their frequent focus on parish concerns. Local NGOs tended to be able to absorb resources, but again had difficulty extending coverage largely due to the problem of financing salaries. Due to their general belief in integrated development, they had shown interest and capability in tackling new sectors, and seemed quite proficient at tacking health services on to existing productive activities. Grassroots organizations showed a surprising degree of investment capacity. They were particularly proficient at serving infrastructure needs that did not entail heavy recurrent costs. They were generally quite good at implementing projects, but only within the restrictive confines of ESF supervision procedures. One important problem that they faced involved shifting membership and a fluctuating quality of leadership.

Assessing the Impact of ESF on NGOs

It is difficult to gauge the impact of the ESF on NGOs due to the short-term nature of the interventions and the difficulty of generalizing about such a varied group of organizations. While the financing of projects undoubtedly allowed many NGOs to expand the range of services they offered, it is unlikely that the basic objectives of these organizations changed in any significant way. Nevertheless, the experience gained by NGOs through their involvement with the ESF in formulating and executing projects was very valuable, and may serve them well as they seek to attract additional resources from external sources in the future.

In budgetary terms, ESF support represented a small portion of NGOs' total financing. This was especially true of local NGOs, international PVOs and, in some respects, of religious organizations. A study carried out on the expenditures in the health sector executed by NGOs in 1988 revealed that ESF financing accounted for only 4 percent of total expenditures that year. Therefore, for most NGOs, the ESF served to reinforce existing programs, but in no way was a decisive factor in the operation of these organizations.

The same was probably not true of grassroots organizations. While no data were available, grassroots organizations had a much reduced access to outside sources of financing. The nature of these organizations was not to establish service networks or on-going programs, but to represent common interests and to press other organizations for assistance and investments. The ESF was surely one of their primary sources of funding. Moreover, the opportunity given to grassroots organizations by the ESF to execute directly a relatively large portfolio of investments was valuable from an institutional-development point of view.

Probably the most significant impact on NGOs of working through the ESF was the maturing of a cooperative relationship with the government. This was most apparent in the health sector, where NGOs signed operational agreements with the government and were ceded entire health districts to operate. In both the health and education sectors, this more integrated relationship took the form of a mixed system, with NGOs administering and providing key investments while receiving inputs in the form of equipment and secondments of technical staff from the Ministry of Health. This model has allowed Bolivia to optimize available resources and plays to each organization's comparative advantage. As a rule, the line ministries lack investment budgets to improve and expand infrastructure and are too centralized to manage decentralized services effectively. However, these agencies are able to assume the recurrent costs of personnel through the national budget process. Likewise, NGOs have a local presence that fosters better management, and through external sources and the ESF, have had access to investment resources. However, NGOs, with their generally unstable cash flows, face their biggest funding challenge in the payment of recurrent costs over the long term.

While progress was made in the coordination of NGO and public agency programs, the progress achieved was fragile. The challenge to the ESF's successor organization, the Social Investment Fund, will be to capitalize on the goodwill generated by the ESF in order to establish concrete mechanisms of coordination through a more complete process of planning and consultation with ministries involved in the financing of health and education projects. However, it is unclear whether at the central level, the government has learned the lessons offered by the ESF in dealing with NGOs. Recently, the central government has reiterated the need to control NGOs and give the state some measure of input in the distribution of external resources to NGOs.

Lessons from the ESF Experience

The Bolivian case has shown that even in a situation where NGOs' attitudes toward the government are skeptical at best, and hostile at worst, steps can nevertheless be taken on a concrete level to bring the government and NGOs into closer cooperation. The movement to closer cooperation requires getting the *mechanisms* right. The importance of working in a technically efficient and transparent manner to win the confidence of NGOs cannot be overstated. In the ESF's case, much of this efficiency and transparency came from its position as an autonomous agency that could not easily be manipulated by the political and organizational interests of the line ministries. Excellent staffing decisions and full logistical support in terms of computers, vehicles, radios and so forth were also essential.

Giving both public and private agencies access to the ESF brought significant advantages. If the ESF had worked only with the public sector, it would have lost much of its sectorial and geographical reach. Because the ESF was open to both public and private agencies, it allowed the public agencies to reach as far as they had the technical and administrative capacity, with the remaining holes in coverage being picked up by NGOs. The NGOs remained at the forefront of providing basic services to the poorer populations in the most remote regions, rather than becoming a competitor of the public sector. Furthermore, if the ESF had been open exclusively to NGOs (as is the plan for several agencies to be created in other countries using the general ESF model), at least one serious "political" problem would have resulted. An exclusive focus on NGOs would have, in all likelihood, exacerbated existing tensions between NGOs and the line ministries, resulting in further efforts by the government to control and inspect NGOs, and in possible sabotage of the ESF from within the public sector.

A further mechanism that ended up being essential to the effective use of NGOs as a channel for ESF financing was the importance the ESF placed on financing projects, not programs. The ESF's operational mechanisms were strong where NGOs tend to be weak. Its practice of financing only carefully itemized budgets of very specific, short-term projects was ideal for working with organizations that often lacked solid internal administrative systems, had shifting membership (in the case of grassroots organizations), and had become accustomed to financing broadly defined programs with external funds that were often spent with few restrictions and in the absence of close supervision by the donor.

The ESF's experience also revealed some of the limitations inherent inworking with NGOs. While NGOs were valid channels for financing, their expansion capacity should not be over-estimated. Local NGOs and international PVOs, which were often viewed as somehow having a capacity to extend coverage wherever it was needed, in fact tended to use the ESF to consolidate existing operations rather than to expand them. This behavior in fact followed from the typical methodology used by NGOs. Their emphasis on developing real community participation and in focusing integrated services on a particular geographical area meant that a longer maturation time was needed before they could consider expansion of services. An additional caveat was that while NGOs were a useful mechanism for extending project benefits to poor populations, relying on NGOs was probably not sufficient to assure reaching the poorest of the poor.

To conclude, one of the most unexpected lessons of the ESF has to do with the dynamism of grassroots organizations in Bolivia. These organizations have usually been viewed as a mechanism for political control or simply as a channel for food aid, or have been eclipsed by the attention given to the organized and savvy local NGOs, PVOs, and religious organizations. Rarely have these organizations been regarded as capable of offering an effective investment channel. The experience with the ESF reveals that grassroots organizations should not be discounted, show a surprising range, represent beneficiaries more directly, and can generate significant amounts of counterpart financing, even in very poor regions.

Notes

1. It should be noted that simultaneously the World Bank was undertaking to establish a dialogue with NGOs in Bolivia to better incorporate the NGO experience into the design and execution of Bank-financed projects. Through time, the major NGOs have recognized the commitment of the World Bank to working with NGOs. Ironically, many NGOs now view the World Bank as something of an arbiter between the NGOs and the Bolivian government.

2. The large share for "other government entities" reflects a distortion since the bulk of this support went to help set up a newly founded agency that was intended to work in a manner similar to the ESF, but which did not present projects for ESF financing.

7

Demand-Driven Funds: Managing Their Conflicts

by John Newman, Margaret Grosh, and Steen Jorgensen

Bolivia's Emergency Social Fund (ESF) is of interest apart from its role in easing the social costs of Bolivia's economic crisis. As a demand-driven fund that has focused on funding small-scale, locally based works, it has provided an innovative means for channelling funds from international organizations and other donors down to small projects implemented by government institutions and non-governmental organizations (NGOs). If, as many believe, local or locally-based institutions are to become increasingly important in the delivery of social services and infrastructure in the developing world, then a close analysis of the demand-driven model that the ESF employed to fund local projects is in order. Drawing partly on the experience of the ESF, and partly on economic theory, this chapter analyzes the economic aspects of a demand-driven fund, and extracts from that analysis a series of recommendations concerning the operation of such a fund.

A Brief Economic Assessment of Demand-Driven Funds

The Cost Structure of Preparing Project Proposals

The experience of the ESF in Bolivia is best understood once one recognizes the cost structure for preparing projects faced by agencies presenting proposals to the ESF, the economic incentives built into the way the ESF was implemented, and the economic problems inherent in introducing a demand-driven fund.

How the Cost Structure Works. Different institutions face varying fixed costs of preparing fundable project proposals. "Fixed costs" are the one-time costs that a prospective recipient of ESF funding would have had to pay the first time it attempted to receive funding. In this context, fixed costs could have involved taking time to learn about the ESF and how it works; this might even have required travelling to La Paz to meet with ESF staff. Taking time to learn how to prepare formal project proposals would have been another important fixed cost. A third fixed cost would have been that of convincing the ESF that the agency requesting funding had the capability to implement well the project for which it was requesting financing. For relatively unsophisticated or remotely-located groups—such as grassroots organizations, NGOs or some municipalities—these fixed costs could have been high. Once these fixed costs were paid, however, the marginal costs[1] of preparing subsequent project proposals (i.e., costs that had to be borne each time a proposal was prepared) were relatively low, principally because the ESF did not impose counterpart funding requirements.[2] Thus the main marginal cost was that of preparing the technical specifications for each project. Most government agencies had staff engineers or architects on their staffs who could do this, though of course it took time away from other activities. NGOs and smaller local governments got around the difficulty by enlisting engineers or architects to do the project formulation on the speculation that if the project was approved, they would be selected by the NGO as the contractor. In either case marginal costs were relatively low, and not usually in financial terms. As will be explained in more detail below, low marginal costs would be expected to generate an excess demand for project funding.

Implications of the Cost Structure. The pattern of funding proposals over time is predictable from the cost structure facing the local agencies. In general, one may expect a delayed reaction to the introduction of a social fund as different local agencies overcome the fixed costs of preparing projects. It may be necessary for the fund to help some agencies to get over the fixed-cost hurdle by providing help with project preparation.[3] Once an organization has made its fixed-cost investment, its strategy in submitting projects will be heavily influenced by the magnitude of the relevant marginal costs. If these costs are relatively low, and organizations seeking funding do not know exactly how funding decisions are made, then the best strategy for them may be to prepare as many projects as possible in the hope that at least one will be funded. In the ESF's case, where marginal costs were low, the demand for funding eventually outstripped the supply. As might have been expected, institutions with lower fixed costs, such as large municipalities and major government agencies that quickly became familiar with the ESF and knew how to submit proposals, provided most of the early funding requests.

Not having a counterpart financing requirement placed a larger administrative burden on the ESF management team than it would otherwise have had. First, without counterpart financing, local agencies had little if any incentive to prescreen projects, thereby placing the full burden of appraisal on ESF staff. Second, supervision problems also could have been reduced if local agencies had more of a stake in the projects. Further, the ESF had to face the potentially adverse political consequences of possibly raising expectations above a level that could be fulfilled with available funding.

Central versus Local Preferences

Differing Preferences. Another feature of the ESF was that in funding projects for implementation by local-level organizations, it promoted the decentralization of the provision of certain services. In principle, this raises the question of how the central funding agency is to go about balancing its interests (in terms of types of projects to be funded) with those of the implementing agencies and the communities they serve. In practice, this issue was recognized, but only superficially addressed, by the ESF, as was to be expected given its limited lifespan and "emergency" orientation. For example, if the central government wants to promote nutrition, and the local agencies want to build soccer fields, mechanisms must be built into the workings of the demand-driven fund to convey the message that nutrition programs are desirable. Without such mechanisms, demand-driven funds are likely to receive an excess of project proposals over available funding (excess demand) in some categories, and fewer proposals than available funds would allow (excess supply) in other categories. This is an outcome attributable partly to the motivation and capability of local agencies to submit proposals, and partly to their preferences in terms of the types of projects they would like to see funded. The way in which the central funding agency ultimately decides to correct the imbalances between supply and demand will determine whether, ultimately, the preferences of the central agency or the local agencies prevail.

Strategic Behavior. The net effect on sectorial investment levels of a fund such as the ESF depends upon the strategic behavior of agencies requesting its financing. The introduction of a fund can have the effect of establishing a differential "price" for projects if there are other sources of funding for similar types of projects. The "price" of the project to the implementing agency is composed of the direct and indirect costs incurred in securing the funding, carrying out the project, supervising its long run operations, and in any reporting requirements. For example, if a social fund makes available financing for health projects with no counterpart financing requirements, and few reporting requirements or quality checks on the services delivered, this is likely to constitute a much cheaper way of financing health projects than existed before.

Consider the case of a regional development corporation (RDC) that raises its own revenue and has its own budget to allocate. It must decide whether to finance a health project out of its own budget or to seek financing from the social fund. The opportunity cost of financing a health project out of its own budget is the value of other projects that financing the health project will preclude. In other words, with a fixed budget, one dollar spent on health precludes one dollar from being spent on something else. Obtaining financing from the social fund for a health project when there is no counterpart financing requirement, on the other hand, would not reduce the amount of money available to the RDC for other investments. Thus, if financing from the social fund is obtained, the RDC's opportunity cost of undertaking the project is zero. This price differential provides an incentive to the RDC to devise a strategy that will allow it to obtain the lowest-cost funding possible for all the projects it wishes to implement. Suppose, for example, that its highest priority project was in the health sector, and that the rest of the projects on its priority list were in other sectors not financed by the fund. A low-cost strategy would have the RDC seek funding for the health project from the fund, and reallocate its own budget to as many as possible of the remaining projects on its list. However, there is always a chance that the request for funding for the health project will be denied. If funding were in fact to be denied, the ironic outcome could be that a high-priority health project that the RDC would have funded in the absence of the fund ends up not being funded at all. The outcome of the RDC's strategic behavior is a sub-optimal distribution of project funding.

Administrative Indicators and Internal Incentives

One essential characteristic of a demand-driven fund is that by inviting demand for project funding, it raises expectations on the part of potential beneficiary groups. If it is to maintain its credibility, the fund has to go a long way toward meeting those expectations. One of the best ways to do so is to disburse as much funding as possible as quickly as possible. The ESF was keenly aware of this need to establish quickly, and then maintain, credibility, because its management knew that few Bolivians were prepared to believe that a government agency would keep its promises. Accordingly, project approval rates were monitored closely. An important performance indicator imposed on ESF staff was the dollar value of projects approved each week.

This choice of the dollar value of projects approved as the key management indicator provided undesirable incentives to ESF staff. First, it resulted in considerable pressure being placed on the appraisal staff to recommend projects of marginal quality, especially in weeks when, for one reason or another, the value of projects submitted to the board of directors for final approval was lower than average. Furthermore, since it required roughly the same amount of work to appraise small projects as large ones, there was a strong incentive for appraisal staff to concentrate their efforts on large projects in major urban areas (which were easily accessible to transport, meaning that the appraiser had to devote less time to making a site visit than if appraising a remote, rural project). Thus appraisal staff tended to focus on proposals for infrastructure undertakings (e.g., street paving) which had been submitted by municipalities or RDCs. The early difficulties that the ESF had in working with NGOs and small community organizations had already made it difficult to find a sufficient number of fundable social assistance projects; the bias toward urban infrastructure projects created by the dollar-based appraisal quota only aggravated the problem. An ad hoc approach was taken to dealing with this issue: occasionally, "sweeps" would be made, during which appraisal staff were told that for a certain period their monetary performance goal would be suspended and they were to focus instead on appraising a backlog of small projects in remote areas.

Recommendations for the Operation of Social Funds

Central versus Local Preferences

As discussed above, a key issue in the design of a fund is how to balance the preferences of the central funding agency against those of the local agencies. If local preferences are not considered at all, then the center would just prepare project plans and seek contractors to carry them out. If, on the other hand, the center's preferences are not considered, then the funding agency would have no real need for project selection criteria. It would just distribute money on some ad hoc basis, until the funds were used up. This section describes some mechanisms for achieving a reconciliation between the two extremes.

Require Counterpart Financing. Social funds may wish to institute a requirement that local agencies provide counterpart financing. This requirement would have three advantages: (a) it would allow the central management team to use differential pricing to induce the local agencies to reveal their own priorities for funding, which would lower the administrative burden of appraisal; (b) it would give the executing agencies more of a stake in the projects and thus tend to reduce implementation problems; and (c) it would bring the distribution of funding requests across the different categories more in line with targeted funding.

The main argument raised against counterpart financing is that many local agencies, particularly NGOs, cannot afford to contribute.[4] This problem can be minimized by allowing the counterpart contribution to be paid in labor, management time or materials, although a counterpart financing requirement might still exclude some poorly endowed organizations.

A theoretical solution would be to give lump-sum transfers to local agencies that they could then use either to finance their own activities or to meet counterpart funding requirements. An advantage of this approach is that it would not alter the marginal costs (in terms of counterpart financing requirements) faced by the groups receiving the transfers. The obvious and overwhelming practical disadvantage is that in deciding to whom to give the lump-sum transfers, the government would have to decide to give certain groups a direct and highly visible form of support, while excluding others. Thus, this approach is likely to be too difficult in most circumstances, both administratively and politically. It could work where government agencies that already receive some form of revenue sharing are eligible for social fund financing.

Impose Differential Counterpart Financing Requirements. Different counterpart financing requirements can convey information to the local agencies about what projects the central agency prefers. In essence, differential counterpart financing requirements constitute different prices for different types of projects. The prices may be set by the center based simply on political preference or on studies that indicate what projects are successful and what investments most increase families' welfare. For example, if studies indicated that irrigation programs rather than road-building appear to be more effective in increasing rural incomes, then the central agency could attach a lower co-financing requirement to irrigation projects than to road building projects. All other things being equal, the lower prices should induce local agencies to propose more irrigation projects. If the local agencies' priorities differ from the central agency's, the local agencies can still submit proposals for the categories with higher counterpart financing requirements. In this way, the local agencies still retain some autonomy. A more flexible outcome is achieved than one in which the center decides all the investments that are to take place in a local area.

If counterpart funding requirements are to be manipulated in such a way as to influence local preferences, local agencies must be in a position to make meaningful choices between different types of projects. This state of affairs is not always present, however. Sectorial ministries, some NGOs or grassroots organizations only undertake one type of activity; some groups only do nutrition programs, others only get involved in water supply projects, etc. The central fund cannot, in the short-term, influence by way of counterpart funding requirements (or other means) the type of work done by these one-dimensional groups.[5] It is only when proposals come from organizations that have a wide variety of activities in their portfolios, that mechanisms for reconciling local and central preferences associated with the differential counterpart financing requirements will come into play.

Equalize Implicit Prices from Different Funding Sources. When a local agency can obtain funds for the same activity from several sources with different implicit costs, it has, as described above, an incentive to engage in strategic behavior that may lead to an undesirable (sub-optimal) outcome. To the extent feasible, therefore, the implicit prices for the same activity funded from different sources should be made as similar as possible. The implicit price is composed of counterpart financing, repayment of funds, cost recovery and reporting requirements. This issue was addressed by the ESF in 1987, soon after it began operations. The municipality of La Paz had just reached agreement with the World Bank on concessional financing for work including street paving, sewerage and erosion control, projects for which funding was also available from the ESF. The terms of the World Bank agreement required that cost recovery measures be put in place in the neighborhoods after the works were completed. To avoid creating a situation in which the municipality would face different financing costs depending on the source of funding, the ESF instituted a rule that a local agency receiving ESF funding would have to impose cost recovery measures identical with those used for similar works of the agency, irrespective of the source of financing.

Project Selection

Set Explicit Targets. Attempting to compare projects in different sectors based on objective criteria would involve complex and often highly subjective calculations of social rates of return. The more practicable approach for a social fund is to make explicit (and more or less arbitrary) decisions at the outset on the proportions of its budget that it wishes to devote to various geographic regions and types of projects. Having done this, it becomes far less costly from an administrative point of view to compare project proposals within a given category than across categories.

Appraise Using a Moving Target. Having chosen the targets and set the cofinancing requirements, there remains the task of choosing among competing proposals within the same category. Choosing to finance one project this month carries with it an opportunity cost of not being able to finance another project in the future. The dynamics of the process are important. A bad project submitted this month should not be financed solely to meet an approval goal when other worthwhile projects will be forthcoming in the near future; rather, the money should be reserved, and more projects approved later.

We propose that projects in any given month be ranked in comparison to projects received over a specified period, say the last three months. This ranking may be ordinal or cardinal. Under this system, if a low quality group of proposals was received in a particular month, they would not be funded because they would fall short of the standard maintained over the preceding three months. If the quality of the proposals received the following month returned to average, then more projects than normal would be funded because the standard of the prior three months would have been lowered by the preceding lot of low quality proposals. This mechanism will smooth out variations in project quality by reducing approvals when bad projects are bunched, and by increasing approvals when good projects are bunched. It would, in so doing, lead to some variation in the amount of approvals per month.

There may be changes over time in the quality distribution of feasible projects. In general an agency will submit its best or highest priority proposals first.[6] For small agencies such as NGOs or small municipalities, the pool of good proposals may be just a few projects and it may be hard to add to this pool. For larger agencies such as the RDCs or branches of ministries, the pool of good projects is much larger because their responsibilities cover wide sector or geographic areas and they have more sophisticated technical staffs to translate needs into projects.

The rolling appraisal standard decision rule would lead to a self-correcting mechanism. If the quality of the available pool falls and the social fund wants to maintain the target financing for the category, then the best strategy would be to accept the best projects out of the available pool, which would occur with the rolling comparison standard.

Unfortunately, the ESF did sometimes slip into the practice of approving less than optimal projects to meet approval goals, principally because it felt under pressure during its start-up period to get as many projects under way as possible. In one instance, the ESF approved a proposal from a municipality for construction of a road along a hillside, though it knew that the same municipality was also doing excavation work in the general vicinity of the planned road site. Not surprisingly, the road caved in not long after it was completed.

The ESF's experience demonstrates both that underlying project quality from any given small organization falls over time, and that the clarity of the project proposal tended to rise. Particularly for the smaller, less sophisticated groups that sought funding from the ESF, a strong learning-curve in the presentation of the project was observed. Initially, although the underlying idea might be very good, the proposals submitted from these groups tended to be of low quality until the technical staff learned how to design and justify projects. On the other hand, the quality of the ideas underlying the project proposals did behave as one would expect. It was evident, for example, for several NGOs operating in Bolivia, that the order in which it submitted proposals to the ESF was closely correlated to the quality of the basic idea behind its proposals.

An observation that the quality of the proposals submitted has fallen is useful information for the management team of the social fund. It suggests that the local agencies have run into diminishing returns in a given category. The social fund should then consider either giving additional technical assistance in the preparation of these projects, reducing the co-financing requirement to induce more submissions, or reducing the amount of funding targeted for this category.

Administrative Considerations

Sequence Commitments. The commitments of the fund should be built up gradually. Otherwise, if the entire sum is available at the beginning, the fund would be rapidly depleted by approving proposals of agencies with the lowest fixed costs of preparing proposals. In the case of the ESF, the gradual build up of the funds available for disbursement occurred automatically as fund-raising took place throughout the implementation of the program. With other funds that may be fully funded before the initial commitment, explicit attention should be given to their sequencing. If the fund has (as the ESF did) a fixed termination date, then commitments should be reduced gradually as termination approaches. Otherwise, there is a risk of making bad decisions under the time pressure of having to disburse remaining funds.

Avoid Perverse Internal Incentives through Choice of Management Indicators. The management indicators used to monitor the fund should not induce biases in project appraisal procedures and standards. Indicators should include both the value and number of projects appraised. Indeed, it may be further desirable to monitor separately the progress of appraisals by sector, region or implementing agency and to assign "bonus" points in sectors where progress is below programmed levels. Using both the value and number of projects avoids introducing incentives to appraise projects at one end of the size spectrum or the other, independent of quality, sector or other considerations. Monitoring the rate of project appraisal rather than approval provides an indicator of administrative performance without inducing undue pressures to approve poor quality projects. This is not to say that the value and number of projects approved would not be monitored; obviously these will be important in measuring project impact and the need for resources in the project supervision department.

Adjustment for Excess Supply and Demand of Funds.

Even if the central funding agency signals its intentions by setting funding targets for each category and differential counterpart financing requirements, it may still find that there are fewer funding proposals than the targeted amount in some categories (excess supply) and more funding proposals than the targeted amount in others (excess demand). In the case of excess supply, the management team of the social fund faces the following options. It may:

- put out bids for projects;
- lower the counterpart financing or subsidize the activity;
- attempt to lower the fixed costs of preparing project proposals;
- lower the standards for appraisal; or
- lower the targeted funding in the category.

In the case of excess demand, the management team may:

- increase the counterpart funding;
- raise the standards for appraisal; or
- increase the targeted funding in the category.

Altering the counterpart financing requirements while holding the target funding fixed is a way to bring the funding proposals closer in line with the preferences of the central government. Altering the funding targets while holding the counterpart financing requirements constant would increase the weight of the local preferences in subsequent outcomes. Of course, any combination of changes to counterpart financing requirements and funding targets is possible.

If the central government wants to have its preferences always dominate the outcomes, and views the local agencies more as executing agencies than as independent groups with possibly conflicting preferences, then clearly, a demand-driven mechanism for generating project proposals is inappropriate. Rather than fine-tuning the incentives to have the local agencies propose exactly what the central agency wants, it would be far more efficient for the central agency to put out competitive bids for the investments it would like to see done.

Recommendations

The main recommendations are as follows:

- Decide to what extent local agencies are to be simply executing agencies for implementing the central government's investment plan or to what extent local preferences are to be considered.
- Impose a counterpart financing requirement on local agencies requesting funding.
- Set different counterpart financing requirements across categories to signal to local agencies the preferences of the funding agency.
- Attempt to harmonize implicit prices charged by various funding agencies (domestic and external) for financing given types of activity.
- Set explicit funding targets for each category of investment and review them periodically in light of past experience.
- Compare projects within a category but not across categories.
- Appraise projects based on how they compare with proposals within the same category submitted over a defined period.
- Set indicators of administrative performance in terms of projects appraised rather than approved, and use numbers of projects as well as their value in the indicators.
- Increase fund disbursements gradually at the beginning of the program and decrease them gradually at the end of the program.

Notes

1. The analogy of an amusement park has been used to explain the fixed-cost/marginal cost structure faced by potential recipients of ESF funding. The cost of the admission ticket to the park (i.e. the fixed costs) may have been relatively high, but once it was purchased, the cost of going on rides in the park (marginal costs) was quite low.
2. The Bolivian ESF did not formally require counterpart financing. Many agencies offered it, nonetheless (see Chapter 6). The presence of counterpart financing influenced the project evaluation process, albeit in a somewhat unsystematic way. In general the presence of counterpart financing was taken as a sign that the soliciting organization would be able to sustain the project's operations once ESF funding expired.
3. This was an important part of what the ESF's promotion department did (see Chapter 1).
4. In fact, Bolivian grassroots organizations were able to generate a surprising amount of counterpart funding (see Chapter 6).
5. But the central agency may be able to influence the level of activity and, through shifting funds among agencies, the overall mix of projects.
6. The quality of the idea of the project should not be confused with the quality of its translation into the ESF's project outline forms. Some very good project ideas were poorly elaborated in the early days of the ESF. Thus when in discussing institutional development it is said that the proportion of appraisal projects rose dramatically during the ESF's life, it refers to the phenomenon of agencies learning to go from the idea "we need a school" to detailing how many bags of cement, how many pounds of nails, how much whitewash, and how many person-months of labor would be needed to build the school.

8

A Hard Act to Follow: The Options

by Mary Barton

As 1988 drew to a close, the "Cinderella clause" of the Emergency Social Fund (ESF) which called for the termination of the ESF at the end of 1989, hung like a cloud over the future. The ESF's management and the project team at the World Bank began to look closely at ESF's successes and failures and to wonder whether it made sense to alter the agency's function and programs. Set up as an emergency institution, the ESF shortcut several bureaucratic norms. These shortcuts included curtailing procedures for procurement, for hiring and firing of staff, and for monitoring of the tax payments of contractors. The exemptions were allowed because the ESF was a "special case" and, in any event, had been planned to last only for three years. As the end of the second year approached, there was considerable pressure on the government and ESF staff to decide what would come next. The ESF had proved a success and many were anxious lest it disappear with no legacy other than the infrastructure it had financed.

As discussions on the future began, several ideas were suggested by various parties from the ESF, the World Bank, the donors and the government of Bolivia. After some consideration, the options were narrowed to four:

- Keep the ESF as is;
- End the ESF;
- Replace the ESF with a permanent institution with a more limited mandate for financing projects only in health and eduction; or
- Expand the role of the management team at the ESF, moving them away from the agency and turning them into a think tank for policy planning.

The Options

Keep the ESF as Is

The argument to leave the ESF unchanged was based on the ESF's success in investing funds in sensible small projects. The logic was "if it ain't broke, don't fix it". For over two years, the ESF had had phenomenal success in investing donors' funds quickly and transparently. In 1985 there had been a tremendous backlog of foreign aid available to the Bolivian government that it was unable to use. The absorptive capacity of the Bolivian economy was extremely low, which was one reason why so many donors put their money behind the ESF when the agency began to spend and spend fast. If the ESF were stopped or changed in any way, time and money would inevitably be lost in the process. In support of this argument, the government had consistently referred to the ESF as a "bridge between the crisis and the reactivation" in the economy. Most agreed that by the end of 1988 the reactivation had not yet taken hold, thus, the "bridge" should stay in place.

Those arguing for change (which included most donors, the World Bank's management and Fernando Romero, the ESF's first executive director) felt that the good times would not last for the ESF. First, it would be difficult for the ESF and Bank staff to continue to justify the shortcuts approved for this temporary institution. On the Bank's side, a particularly contentious issue was that the ESF's first loan not only allowed very lenient procurement regulations, but also the ESF had twice requested and been granted exceptions even to those. Just as one procurement problem was solved, another would appear. In neither case did it appear that the ESF was deliberately trying to get around the rules; nonetheless, these breaches did not bode well for the future of the agency.

A second strong argument against letting the ESF continue unchanged was that even the agency's strongest supporters recognized the need to integrate better its work with that of the social sector ministries. Coordination would ensure that the ESF's investments were consistent with the various sectors' policies, strategies and investment plans. As long as the ESF did not adequately coordinate its projects with the line ministries' investment plans, there was bound to be some overlapping coverage (duplicate health centers outside Santa Cruz are an example). Also, it was possible that the priorities identified by the ESF might not be the same as those identified by the ministries or their counterparts at the departmental level. Finally, the projects financed by the ESF were for the most part not included in the Public Investment Program. The ESF produced guidelines for the type of projects that it would like to see submitted, but could not predict exactly what type of projects would, in fact, be submitted. As the volume of investment channelled through the ESF began to increase, government officials began to worry that all of this represented unprogrammed investment.

Third, though the "demand-driven" design of the ESF had been successful in capturing community support, the neediest communities were not submitting projects. To continue to channel a large portion of public investment through an organization with only rudimentary targeting procedures was undesirable once the crisis lessened.

The benefits of creating a new institution were evident as soon as the ESF started to operate effectively, but by the end of 1988 some of the problems with adding a new institution to the bureaucracy were beginning to show.

End the ESF

The primary argument for terminating the ESF was that it had been established as an temporary institution and should not be allowed to become permanent. To extend the life of the ESF might mean that the various agencies for which it was substituting would never develop their own capacity for investing in small projects. The ESF was a new institution and its mission overlapped with those of the health and education ministries at the very least. In the short run, these ministries clearly did not have the institutional capacity for implementing investment projects in addition to generating policy and keeping administrative control of the corresponding sector. In the long run, however, Romero and his staff recognized the dangers of creating new institutions where old ones were not functioning. Bolivia did not need a burgeoning bureaucracy. It also did not make sense to have the investment arm for the social sectors in a separate and independent institution.

The donor community, which had responded so well to the "emergency," might well lose interest in the ESF. The ESF had been a hot topic for some time and one of the keys to Bolivia's future, but now it was old news and the donors were growing restless. It was not a "sexy" enough project anymore. If the donors were to lose interest, the ESF could not continue to disburse money at its customary rapid pace because the government would be unable to pick up the slack. Instead of risking the financial demise of the ESF, some donors advocated shutting down the institution while it was still on top.

The ESF's independent status meant that the executive director reported only to the president and not to any other cabinet minister. Naturally, ESF's success led to some jealousy within the government, which made it increasingly difficult for the organization's directors to operate independently, approving projects based only on their merit and not on the desires of any particular ministry or political group. Some ministers began to question the ESF's independent status, while others began to vie to have the ESF placed under the auspices of their own ministry.

By the end of 1988, signs began to develop that national politics were finally beginning to interrupt the usually clean and efficient business of the ESF. Presidential elections were set for May of 1989. All of the three serious contenders to succeed Paz Estenssoro supported the continuation of the New Economic Policy (the adjustment package), and all supported the work of the ESF. But, all of them were also anxious to claim part of the credit for the ESF's success. The ESF was naturally identified with the party in power, the MNR, but the party on the left (MIR) and the party on the right (ADN) both had people working at the ESF as directors and on the board of directors. If the MNR admitted that the government was going to go through with closing the ESF at the end of 1990, it would clearly provide its opponents with political ammunition. Meanwhile, the ESF lost its politically adept executive director, Fernando Romero, when he was appointed to be Minister of Planning.

Even more worrisome than national politics was the pressure of the upcoming local elections. Suddenly, if one province had the ESF's support in rehabilitating a provincial hospital, every province wanted a similar project to be approved. In some instances, tremendous pressure was put on the staff of the ESF to approve projects that they knew were outside of the priorities and guidelines that they themselves had set for the agency. In most cases, the staff resisted the pressure and became even more selective about which projects were approved. Nonetheless, the precedent for political interference in the ESF was set, and the potential for increasing interference worried many of the donors and the staff at the World Bank.

Despite these concerns which cast a shadow over the future of the ESF, most people involved did not want to see the institution closed down. The staff at the ESF did not want to see all of their hard work in developing the systems used by the ESF for identifying, appraising and monitoring projects to go to waste. The government did not want its most successful undertaking to wind down (particularly not in an election year). And the donors, though they were anxious for new and fresh approaches, were reluctant to close an operation that ensured the absorption of foreign aid in a country where this had always been problematic.

Replace the ESF with a Circumscribed Permanent Institution

Some at the ESF, including Romero, argued that those ministries that could take over the relevant project areas should do so. The ESF could provide technical assistance in helping them to adopt more efficient systems of identification, appraisal and monitoring. The permanent version of the ESF should continue to work only where it was most needed and the danger of inefficient duplication of effort was least.

Under the Ministry of Transportation, for example, there already existed an agency responsible for rural road projects. This agency had supervised most rural road projects financed under the ESF. With the proper technical assistance, the staff at the ESF felt that this agency could return to identifying, appraising and financing its own projects. It had gained experience in working with the ESF projects, and in most cases had been very effective in supervising them. Similarly, it was hoped that responsibility for lower income housing projects, could be transferred back to the National Housing Fund under the Ministry of Urban Affairs. There was some skepticism about the Housing Fund's ability to execute projects efficiently, but since this was its reason for existing, the agency needed to develop the capacity. Significant technical assistance from the ESF could be provided to improve the agency's ability to appraise and monitor projects.

The handful of production projects, which were mostly rotating credit funds for small enterprises, could be transferred to one of the new funds that had sprung into existence during the preceding year called the Peasant Development Fund. And, still another fund, called the Regional Development Fund, would be able to absorb projects in water, irrigation and sewerage. These funds could work closely with the ESF to copy its systems of project and financial management; in fact, a former departmental director of the ESF had been named to head the Peasant Development Fund and took two years of experience working to develop the ESF with him. The only problem with these funds was that nobody was quite sure whether they would survive the 1989 elections. Many people thought that they were a ploy to gain favor for the government party during an election year. On the other hand, the Bolivians saw that they had something that worked in the ESF and were tempted to replicate it to the greatest extent possible.

With the preceding transfers delineated, the ESF would be left projects only in education and health, including some small-scale water and sewerage. The ministries in these sectors were notoriously weak and inept in identifying or supervising investment projects. Also, the Ministries of Health and Education spent over 90 percent of their recurrent budgets on salaries, with the result that their planning and development capacity was very limited.

With a reduced sectorial portfolio, the ESF would be able to specialize in developing its project selection criteria and to coordinate planning more closely with the respective ministries. The narrower focus would also give the ESF more time to work with communities in isolated rural areas to generate projects where the poorest of the poor live. Finally, when the time came that the Ministries of Health and Education were ready to handle their own investment projects, the transfer of systems and personnel into the ministries would be easier. In the meantime, the ESF would have a new face and the old reliability, a combination certain to be attractive to donors.

Expand the Role of the Management Team at the ESF

The directors at the ESF had been so successful that everyone at the Bank was preoccupied with keeping this talented group of young people working in the public sector, preferably as a team. Senior management at the World Bank suggested in one of the first meetings called to discuss the future of the ESF, that this group of leaders should be transferred to the Ministry of Planning where they would sit in a council slightly separate from the ministry and above the minister and generate ideas for development across the sectors. They would act as an elite policy group, suggesting ideas to be implemented by the Ministry of Planning, and keeping watch over the planning activities of all the line ministries.

The primary objection to this idea within the Bank was that it would certainly be rejected by the Bolivians. Although this team had proven effective in managing the ESF, its members were still quite young, and the ministers already viewed them as upstarts. Moreover, none of the directors really had a background in policy planning. Their work at the ESF had actually involved very little work in policy planning and no macroeconomics. They were brilliant at finance and at overcoming operational difficulties, but as they were the first to admit, they were not trained policymakers.

The Plan

As described in the next chapter, the Bolivians choose the third option of dismantling the ESF in part while replacing it with a new institution that would fund health and education projects. Thus, in a sense, the institution was not as "temporary" as originally advertised. Its successor, the Social Investment Fund, will carry on in the medium term. Ideally, in another few years, the Social Investment Fund will also undergo a transformation; one in which it will be absorbed into stronger Ministries of Health and Education. If this can be accomplished, and the ESF's systems transferred and applied successfully, the ESF will have been a truly temporary institution with a permanent sustainable impact on the social sectors in Bolivia.

9

After the ESF: The Social Investment Fund as Successor

by Constance Sepeda

In order to carry forward the work of the Emergency Social Fund (ESF), which it judged successful, the government of Bolivia established the Social Investment Fund (SIF) as the ESF's successor. The SIF is meant to build on the ESF, and to improve upon it in several respects. The rationale behind the decision was explained in the preceding chapter. Here, the elements of the fledgling SIF are outlined.

The Social Investment Fund

Objectives

In contrast with the ESF's emphasis on employment creation, the SIF is geared to contribute to Bolivia's long term growth through human capital formation. Specifically, it aims to:

- extend coverage of health, education, and water and sanitation services to reach more of the poor in Bolivia;
- provide a coordinating link with the many agencies active in the social sectors, including them as participants (project requesters, implementers, and supervisors) in its program; and
- increase external assistance to the social sectors by providing an efficient, transparent mechanism for donors to contribute to priority investments in health and education.

Organizational Structure and Staffing

Like the ESF, the SIF was established with legal autonomy under the direct oversight of the President of the Republic. The SIF's board of directors includes one more member than did ESF: the Under-Secretary of Planning for Social Policy, to support coordination with line ministries. The board of directors is charged with establishing the SIF's internal structure, work programs, and procedures; approving all projects for SIF financing; and presenting semi-annual reports of the SIF's activities to the government. The SIF's executive director is supported by a deputy director, three operational departments (Health, Education, and Supervision), four administrative departments (Legal Affairs, Fund-raising, Administration and Information), and two units (Auditing and Technical Control) that report directly to the executive director. SIF will have a professional staff of about 100 people.

Programming

While the capacity of the ESF was determined primarily by the level of international support available, the SIF's programming will be mainly a function of the capacity of the social sectors to absorb investment. Once fully operational, the SIF expects to commit about $40 million annually to projects in health and education (compared with $23 million committed annually by ESF in those sectors). Average project size is expected to be $70,000 as was the case with the ESF.

Exemptions from Procurement and Civil Service Regulations

Exemption from normal public procurement practices, and freedom to pay staff salaries well above the range of standard public service pay scales were two important factors that contributed to the success of the ESF. It is therefore worth considering how these issues were dealt with by the SIF's designers. In the case of procurement, in spite of the fact that the SIF had been granted an exemption from normal bidding procedures for all contracts costing less than $100,000, SIF's Administrative Council decided that competitive bidding would be required for all contracts. Procurement agents will be engaged for contracts over $100,000[1]; the SIF will oversee the procurement of contracts valued at less than that amount. The SIF, as did the ESF, will maintain a list of unit costs to use as a reference in evaluating bids and will reserve the right to reject all bids offered for any contract, in the event that they substantially exceed the cost estimate based on reference prices.

As for the ESF, the SIF's ability to attract high quality personnel is considered essential to ensure its success. Accordingly, staff will again be hired under fixed-term contracts outside the civil service system and their salaries will be paid from external sources. The government is unable to finance salaries above the civil service scale because of the general constraint on counterpart funds owing to the need for fiscal austerity and the lack of civil service reform. Bolivian law precludes the government from paying salaries above the civil service scale, and public employees from receiving incremental salaries or benefits from non-governmental sources. In the long run, it is planned that the government will restructure the civil service salary scale. In the interim (4 to 5 years) a separate World Bank-financed project has set up a fund to finance key government personnel from external sources. The SIF's salaries will be in line with those of the elite cadre of personnel in other government institutions whose salaries are financed by this fund. Thus the SIF will be able to attract the requisite high quality staff, while being less of an exception within government.

Improving on the ESF's Shortcomings

The SIF, with its longer term perspective and tighter sectorial focus, seeks to improve upon the ESF in four important areas - targeting, project selection, project sustainability and inter-agency coordination.

Poverty Targeting. SIF's major target population is defined as communities with a majority of the population with rates of infant mortality greater than 170 per 1,000 live births and illiteracy over 40 percent of the adult population (lack of data precludes use of family income as a defining variable).

Each project presented for the SIF would be screened at three levels: First, its general geographical location would be considered and checked against available survey data or poverty maps. Second, if a community profile does not already exist in the data base, one would be developed based on a site visit by SIF staff; the profile would include information regarding factors such as climatic zone, resource base, existence and quality of infrastructure (especially for health (including sanitation) and education), basic services, the economic base, and general socio-cultural factors. Third, the proposed project itself would be appraised in terms of its intended beneficiary group, in comparison with the assessment of priority needs generated by the community profile.

The more difficult problem in targeting benefits concerns reaching those communities that have no advocate organization to formulate and request projects. To address this problem, several provinces characterized by acute poverty will be selected on the basis of the poverty maps currently available. The SIF will then identify organizations already working within those provinces and assess their potential for expanding their activities into underserved communities, as well as their capacity for implementing projects. Promotional efforts would then be directed through these organizations, with assistance provided as necessary in the formulation of project proposals. Support may be provided to assist qualified agencies in extending their operations to target areas.

In the short term, there will be an unavoidable gap in targeting efforts, resulting from the fact that critically poor communities will not be included in the first phase of promotional efforts, as a result of limitations of data to identify them, or because their remoteness of location combined with a relatively small population may make the cost of delivering services prohibitive. Nevertheless, the mechanisms should make possible both the prevention of "leakage" of benefits to relatively well-off areas, and extension of benefits to an increasing percentage of the neediest among the poor.

Project Selection. The justification of an SIF project is that it will contribute to improving the health and education of Bolivia's poor. Thus while the project appraisals will cover many of the same points, the focus of the SIF is narrower, and the rigor in selections should be higher. SIF appraisal criteria revolve around the following general principles:

- provision for subproject operation maintenance beyond the project period, including recovery of operating costs by the operating agency where appropriate;
- adherence to norms established by the Ministries of Health or Education where applicable; and
- site visits, and assessment of the institutional capacity of the requesting agency and of the proposed project supervisor.

In addition, appraisal criteria for specific types of projects include:

- for water and sanitation projects, economic analysis, including rate-of-return calculation;
- for social assistance, school construction, and health cost construction, an assessment of cost effectiveness as reflected in their cost per beneficiary; and
- for subprojects involving construction, adherence to norms for appropriate waste disposal and environmental impact in general.

Project Sustainability. The SIF will require that requesting agencies (RAs) provide evidence of their ability to maintain operation of the requested project beyond the period of SIF assistance as one of the criteria of project selection. For many types of projects, such plans would be based in part on application of user fees, although support from other sources is also envisioned. The total cost of each project involving construction would include items to be contributed by the beneficiaries, generally in the form of land, labor, and materials. The exact proportion of beneficiary contribution to investment would vary by project type and the assessed resources of the beneficiaries. RAs would also contribute to subproject cost, usually in cash. Where appropriate and feasible, plans to involve beneficiaries themselves in the maintenance of physical infrastructure would be encouraged. In particular, mechanisms would be developed with the help of technical assistance to facilitate the management of maintenance and operation of water supply and basic sanitation infrastructure by beneficiaries themselves.

Inter-Agency Coordination. In contrast to the ESF, which operated quite independently, the SIF's overall strategy and plan would be presented to the National Council for Social Policy (CONAPSO), of which the SIF's executive director is a member. In developing its annual operational budget, which would be fully articulated within the annual public investment program, SIF's management would establish geographic priorities based on its poverty targeting methodology and would agree on these priorities with the Ministries of Health and Education. For those projects for which government funds would be needed as counterpart during project execution to cover recurrent costs thereafter, final approval of the subproject by the corresponding ministry would be required. Following up on the positive experience of the ESF, the SIF would assure that projects carried out by NGOs are not only consistent with sector priorities, but also conform to government norms (incorporated into SIF's subproject appraisal guidelines) for design, scale and quality. SIF would work through existing networks of NGOs, to avoid the duplication of activities and effort that has occurred among NGOs operating in the same area.

The ESF developed an efficient, computer-based management information system, used mainly to track physical and financial progress of the more than 7,000 subprojects submitted for its consideration. The equipment and software would be shared with SIF in 1990 and transferred to SIF upon ESF's closing. Under SIF, a Directorate of Information has been established, with the responsibility to expand the scope of information management to include full monitoring of the processing of subproject proposals, supervision of subproject execution, and maintenance of internal monitoring indicators, such as average time spent at each stage of processing, and data such as commitments, disbursements, and average cost per beneficiary organized by subproject type. The system would also be used for the establishment and maintenance of "community profiles"; sets of social indicators on communities where ESF- or SIF-financed projects have been, or will be, carried out. Indicators would be used to reflect the number and type of beneficiaries of each type of subproject, such as the number of children by age group receiving text books, vaccinations, and school lunches, in order to monitor real benefits provided under SIF subprojects.

The Costs of Improvements. The SIF's enhanced targeting, project selection, and coordination mechanisms will necessarily lead to slower project promotion and appraisal than the ESF's and therefore to a somewhat higher proportion of administrative costs to total program cost. The SIF's ratio will be between 4 and 5 percent, whereas the ESF's was about 3 percent. Thus, viewed in the short term, the SIF may appear to be less "efficient" than the ESF. From a medium-term perspective, however, it is considered well worth the investment to permit the SIF to correct some of the ESF's shortcomings in terms of targeting, quality and sustainability of investments, and integration of programming into the public expenditure program.

Notes

1. This is standard practice for projects over $30,000 in the rest of the public sector.

10

Who Needs an ESF?

by Steen Jorgensen

More than twenty countries are presently setting up institutions inspired, in part, by the Emergency Social Fund (ESF). As discussed in Chapter 11, the successes and shortcomings of the ESF were to a large degree predictable from its initial design and institutional setup. It is therefore very important to analyze precisely what are the problems to be addressed, what activities can be undertaken, and which organizational arrangements are acceptable prior to undertaking an ESF-type program.

In deciding whether to create something like the ESF, three fundamental questions should be asked. First, what are the goals of the institution? Second, which methods will be used to reach the target groups? Third, what structure is desirable? These questions are interrelated and this chapter assesses under which combination of answers an institution like the ESF would be preferred.

An institution like the ESF is most appropriate to alleviate the costs for the poor of an economic crisis where existing infrastructure and institutions are weak or non-existent. ESF-type institutions are *not* well suited to deal with some direct victims of adjustment, e.g., the laid-off civil servants. To get the best results, an appropriate mix of labor intensive infrastructure rehabilitation and social services should be supported through an institution using a demand-driven approach with sufficient independence to allow "cutting red tape" and working with a broad spectrum of implementing agencies. In any case, many countries may wish to adopt the basic principle of a financial intermediary providing grants to local groups on a demand-driven basis using flexible and well-designed management strategies.

The Goal

The conventional wisdom that has grown up around the ESF might lead one to conclude that an organization like it could be put to any one of the following purposes:

- alleviate the social costs of adjustment or economic crisis;
- alleviate poverty;
- create employment;
- create infrastructure; or
- serve as a mechanism for decentralization.

This section will discuss to what extent an organization like the ESF is a suitable tool to achieve each of these goals.

Coping with the Social Costs of Adjustment or Crisis

Although the ESF is discussed most often under the rubric of "alleviating the social costs of adjustment," it is worth remembering that the Bolivians themselves were not thinking in those terms. They had a broader goal in mind: coping with the social devastation wrought by the economic crisis that gripped the country from 1980 through late 1985. The Supreme Decree issued by the Bolivian government in November 1986 creating the ESF spoke, in general terms, of establishing:

> Mechanisms needed to create employment conditions that will help alleviate the current social crisis, as reflected in the unemployment situation and in health and nutrition indicators, until the goals of the New Economic Policy (i.e., the macroeconomic stabilization and adjustment program launched a year earlier) are achieved.

Fernando Romero, the first executive director of the ESF, has pointed out that the concept of the social costs of adjustment was not foremost in the minds of the designers of the ESF. Instead it was plain to them that Bolivia's poorest citizens had suffered tremendously during the economic crisis, and that the country had lost perhaps a decade of development during that period. The situation, socially and politically, had become explosive. The standard government agencies were themselves effectively paralyzed by years of economic turmoil and general bureaucratic stasis, and were unable to fulfill the needs of the country's people, especially the urgent, basic needs of the poor.

The ESF was set up to shelter the poor, through the creation of jobs and infrastructure, until Bolivia's adjustment program had helped restore incomes and the capacity of the regular state institutions to produce and finance services and infrastructure. This mandate was captured nicely by the ESF's slogan: "The bridge between the crisis and the reactivation." The ESF's focus was clearly not on attempting to identify the social costs of the adjustment program, nor to target its benefits to persons directly affected by the fiscal austerity measures.[1] Thus, while the external agencies that became involved with the ESF chose to regard it as dealing with the social costs of adjustment, this was not what the founders of the ESF had in mind.

Although this could not have been known at the time, recent work has shown that whatever the social costs of adjustment were, they were not borne primarily by the poor. Spending on social programs increased after the implementation of the stabilization program, investment picked up, the poor were taxed less heavily as the regressive inflation tax disappeared, real wages increased substantially and the proportion of urban incomes accounted for by the rich declined.

In general, institutions like the ESF are not well suited to dealing with the narrow social costs of structural adjustment. Most often, the people directly affected by adjustment or stabilization measures are public sector employees who have been fired as part of a program to reduce the public sector deficit. Such people are hard to reach via employment programs, as was seen in Bolivia for laid off employees of the state-owned mining company. These people will generally not accept low-skilled, low-wage jobs as those offered in a labor intensive reconstruction program like the ESF's. Bolivia opted to deal with the laid-off employees by offering substantial severance payments, handing out $60 million to 21,000 miners, an amount that was equivalent, on a per capita basis, to about twice the median annual earnings of an urban worker. Such payment schemes or, alternatively, retraining programs such as those that have been undertaken in Mexico are probably a better solution where retrenched public servants are concerned.

Persons who have always been poor, irrespective of adjustment efforts, are probably more reachable by ESF-style institutions. Targeting jobs to particular groups affected by the adjustment program may be difficult, if not impossible, if the ESF route of relying on private contractors is followed. Enforcing hiring requirements on private contractors is problematic, especially during an adjustment program that aims to reduce the role of the government in the provision of goods and services. This factor made the "automatic" targeting mechanisms relied upon by the ESF all the more appropriate. The relatively low wages offered for most of the jobs at ESF-funded projects ensured that, generally speaking, only poorer workers would apply (Chapter 4).

Poverty Alleviation

Poverty alleviation is a long-run activity comprised of both policies and projects. It is thus not well handled by a temporary institution like the ESF. The ESF was involved in project implementation but not policy formulation. As discussed, the idea of the ESF was to let adjustment-generated growth combined with better redistributive policies alleviate structural poverty and create permanent employment. The ESF was intended to allow the poor to survive until these policies were effective, to improve the country's infrastructure to give greater effect to the new economic policies and to boost implementation capacity. Demand-driven institutions like the ESF can still be an important component of a poverty alleviation strategy, but only one component.

Employment Creation

At any given moment, the ESF provided about 20,000 workers with temporary employment. This was not enough to lower substantially the open unemployment rate, nor the underemployment problem. Also, the jobs were temporary - the average project lasted only five months and most laborers worked on a daily contract. Thus the ESF was not a long run solution to unemployment. Instead it was more like a transfer program that used a work requirement to target beneficiaries, or a labor-intensive infrastructure creation program. To the extent that the ESF helped resolve the unemployment problem, it was through a boost to the demand for labor (that could have occurred through other investment or expenditure channels with low import content) and the limited on-the-job training it provided. Countries wishing to address unemployment head-on would be better advised to put in place sound macroeconomic policies, e.g., ensure that regulation, taxation, and exchange rate policies do not seriously skew the choice of technology away from labor. ESF-type activities could be an important short-run addition to such policies, but not a solution by themselves.

Infrastructure Creation

The strong emphasis placed by the ESF on funding projects that would build economic or social infrastructure was appropriate in Bolivia, where so little infrastructure was in place, where what did exist was generally in poor repair, and where the institutions charged with building and servicing the infrastructure were as inadequate as the infrastructure itself. The ESF model is not appropriate where well-developed infrastructure or institutions are already present (e.g., middle income countries such as Mexico, Chile or Argentina). Even where the ESF model is appropriate in the short run, procedures to integrate more adequately the creation of infrastructure with planning, budgeting and the provision of services that use the infrastructure would be needed in the long run.

A Mechanism for Decentralization

The ESF proved to be an effective channel for revenue sharing and decentralization. The simple fact that the central government made substantial amounts available to local and regional agencies based on clear technical criteria instead of the traditional criteria based on patronage provided a boost to decentralization. The fact that funding levels were decided based upon the quality of submitted proposals, created an important incentive for institutional improvements. Such a learning process was evident, especially in weaker entities. This improved capacity for project preparation stays with the requesting agency even after the ESF program has ended (Chapter 3). These aspects of the ESF's operation may be replicable even in countries that choose other ways of addressing issues of adjustment, poverty, social safety nets, employment and infrastructure creation.

A related concern that has often been raised with the ESF-experience is the need to integrate the social funds' activities into the line ministries in the longer run. This view assumes that it is the function of, for instance, the Ministry of Health to manage all construction of health posts across a country. In contrast with this, many countries (often supported by donors) are trying to make line ministries into normative, policy setting entities and get them out of project implementation. Project implementation is being moved to local or regional authorities. An ESF-type institution could be an important first step in moving project implementation out of line ministries, forcing the ministries to focus on policy-making and sectoral planning. In this aspect an ESF-type institution could become an important vehicle for decentralization.

The Method

After it has been decided to shelter the poor from the effects of some calamity (be it an earthquake, structural adjustment or a profound crisis), the best method should be found. In the provision of a safety net, the question of whether those it catches are the "new" poor (those affected by the adjustment program itself), or the long standing poor is less of an issue. The purpose of a safety net is to help (at least some of) the poor, regardless of the reason for their poverty. The range of methods includes:

- generation of employment in the public sector;
- generation of employment in the private sector; and
- distribution or subsidization of foods, medicines or other essential goods.

Public or Private Employment

In Bolivia, contrary to the experience in other countries, it was decided not to hire people into the public sector. The private sector orientation and its status as a financial intermediary was one of the keys to the ESF's success. It allowed the program to be implemented quickly, kept the program within the spirit of the adjustment program, gave one segment of the private sector a much needed boost after the devastating crisis, and avoided pressures for permanent employment that would have been present in the public sector. On the other hand, working through the public sector could possibly have allowed somewhat finer targeting through the selection of workers, if an efficient screening mechanism were available.

Goods or Wages

Many social safety nets distribute food, medicine or other goods rather than provide employment. The arguments in favor of the distribution of foods, medicines, or other goods rather than of income through employment are as follows: First, intra-household allocation issues, i.e., ensuring that the benefits of the distribution program reach mothers and children as well as the primarily male wage-earners. This can be partially resolved in goods-distribution programs by giving the goods directly to the intended beneficiary, if the intended beneficiary does not pass on the goods, and no substitution takes place.[2] With wage-distribution (employment) programs, the direct beneficiary will usually be a male head of household, and little can be done from the outside to ensure an equitable distribution of benefits within the household. Second, only a portion of the wage income distributed will be spent on food, thereby reducing the benefit if the predominant goal of the program is to generate increased food consumption among the poor. Third, transfer programs can have a lower overhead-to-total cost ratio than employment programs. Even labor-intensive projects require enough materials, skilled labor and administration, that the wages paid may not be the largest element of costs.[3]

These arguments in favor of food distribution imply that the central planner knows the individual's needs better than the individual, an assumption generally rejected by economists. If the individual receives free food she/he may purchase less food and use the money saved for other wants. If the amount of food distributed exceeds what the recipient wants, then the household will sell the extra food (probably at a price substantially below cost), and accrue a benefit less than the central planner intended. In either case, the individual has thwarted the planner's efforts, and the program has incurred higher than necessary costs for the benefit received.

Originally, goods-distributing schemes were also considered instead of the ESF. Such schemes were rejected due to the arguments raised in the preceding paragraph, and due to the following specific problems such schemes would have had in Bolivia: First, they require a good distribution mechanism that was absent in Bolivia. Second, food distribution would have had to be based on donated food and thus could have provided a disincentive to local production. Third, hand-outs of goods would run against the grain of the market-oriented adjustment program implemented in Bolivia, which aimed to reduce the role of the "paternalistic" state. Fourth, the handouts may have long-term positive impact on human capital formation, but the employment program achieved that *and* began to improve Bolivia's deficient physical capital as well.

The Structure

If it is deemed desirable to set up ESF-type institution the basic institutional setup should be decided. The more important issues that would have to be resolved are:

- Will the organization work with public or private sector groups, NGOs, grassroots organizations, or other bodies?
- Will the organization be embodied in an existing institution, or will an entirely new institution have to be created?
- Should the organization be temporary or permanent?

- Should the organization be demand-driven, or should it have a top-down, "command" orientation?

Organizational Framework

In Bolivia, it was decided to work with the whole range of institutions; grassroots groups, local and foreign NGOs, religious organizations, and local, regional, and central government agencies. The primary focus was on projects. If a good project was proposed, and an institution (or institutions) capable of implementing and supervising it was found, then the project was approved irrespective of the politics or religion of the institutions.

Political factors might make this sort of arrangement impossible in many countries. Some governments might not be able to accept that a religious group, or an NGO related to an opposition party or based in a foreign country, should provide education and health services with government support. Besides, there might simply be an acute shortage of effective local groups. These are difficult and sensitive issues, but in the ESF's case, the fact that it worked with a multitude of implementing agencies was clearly one of the keys to its success.

New or Existing Institutions

In Bolivia, public sector institutional capacity sufficient to implement a program on the scale of the ESF simply did not exist in 1986. A new institution had to be created, one that allowed for simplifications in procurement practices and freedom to pay its staff salaries competitive enough to attract high quality staff. The ESF's status as a new agency located outside normal bureaucratic channels allowed it to respond quickly to the expressed needs of communities. Still, it raised the standard problems of competition for scarce management talent, rivalry with existing ministries, and concerns about how it should fit into the planning, budgeting, and coordination process of government.

Temporary or Permanent

The ESF's temporary nature helped to minimize these concerns of placing a new institution in their government structure. It will often be the case that a temporary institution will have an easier time getting many of the exceptional working conditions needed to implement an emergency program. On the other hand, its temporary status is presently causing problems in assuring a smooth transfer of responsibility back to the relevant, permanent public agencies.

Demand-Driven or Top-down

A demand-driven institution is subject to the whims of its potential beneficiary population and to the capacity of preparing and executing agencies, and therefore will not provide perfect targeting. If more precise targeting is feasible with the information available to central planners, its desirability will have to be evaluated. The advantages of precise targeting are obvious. The disadvantages are that it is likely to raise administrative costs substantially, increase turn-around times, and lose the advantages in supervision and sustainability brought by local "ownership" of projects.

Conclusions

Institutions like the ESF are appropriate when:

- A country is in an emergency and needs quick and tangible results;
- the emergency is of a temporary nature, e.g., policies are in place that will ensure growth and redistribution in the medium to long term;
- the country needs a social safety net and needs to rehabilitate its infrastructure;
- the institution can be allowed to work with as broad a range of institutions as possible;
- there are no existing public sector institutions that could do the job;
- overall policies favor private sector development; and
- a willingness exists to accept market based solutions, i.e., when there is not a "the planner knows best attitude".

The worse the country's poverty, infrastructure, and institutional capacity, the more the trade-offs in targeting and coordination made in the ESF will be worthwhile in exchange for immediate, positive impacts. It is worth repeating, that countries in circumstances other than those listed here may address better their poverty, unemployment or social problems through other kinds of programs. Even when many features of the ESF are being replicated, improvements or modifications should be made to tailor the program to the specific needs and requirements of the country.

Whether to create a new institution or use an existing one, and whether to have the program be temporary or permanent, both depend on the country's particular circumstances. A new institution will be more desirable the lower general institutional capacity is. A temporary institution will be desirable when its procedures vary widely from those of the rest of the public sector, or where improvement in the capacity of the rest of the public sector is expected within a short time.

This chapter has discussed when it would be appropriate to duplicate all or most of the ESF's characteristics. It is important to note, however, that some aspects could be replicated under less stringently defined circumstances. The basic principle of a financial intermediary that provides grants to local groups on a demand-driven basis using flexible and well-designed management strategies is more globally applicable. Many of the social funds set up in Africa have adopted such principles for the management of social programs. For example, a recently begun program in Zambia has taken these aspects of the ESF experience and adopted them in managing community development efforts. Such agencies may still be successful in meeting their objective even without the circumstances found in the ESF: a relationship with an adjustment program, a sunset clause, a focus on temporary employment, functioning as a transfer program with a work requirement, and the sense of urgency.

Notes

1. Except for an initial and largely unsuccessful attempt to force contractors to hire ex-employees of the state mining company who were laid off to stop the drain on fiscal resources.
2. Some studies have found that food supplementation programs are less effective than intended, as the children who receive a meal outside the home receive less food at home.
3. This was not the case for the ESF as the direct and indirect wage costs were in the range of two-thirds of total cost. This estimate is based on ESF's administrative records, which include the direct labor cost. To this cost is added the implicit labor cost involved in producing the locally produced materials.

11

In Brief: Successes and Shortcomings

by Margaret Grosh and Steen Jorgensen

This chapter summarizes very briefly the main successes and shortcomings of the Emergency Social Fund (ESF). Opinions on the ESF are mixed. It accomplished a great deal quickly and concretely. When judged against the standards of other development projects, or the effectiveness of most Bolivian public sector agencies, the ESF compared very favorably. It did, however, have shortcomings and when judged against ideal standards was found lacking.

The World Bank's internal evaluations department rated the first ESF project among only 3 "very satisfactory" projects in a comparison of 27 World Bank-funded social sector projects evaluated in 1990. The ESF rated high on all scores (overall status, sustainability and institutional development). This is remarkable given the fact that high ratings are usually correlated with the overall development (as measured by GDP) of the country. The support to the ESF was one of only two projects where credit funds were disbursed on time.

The ESF's Successes

The ESF has raised considerable interest because it has acted quickly and efficiently to produce visible, positive results in a wide variety of areas. In short, the ESF:

- funded over 3,000 small projects in a fast, efficient and transparent way (see Chapter 1);
- raised the incomes of workers on ESF projects substantially (Chapter 4);
- provided high return social and economic infrastructure for the poor (Chapters 1 and 3);

- provided social services to the poor (Chapters 1, 3 and 6);
- attracted substantial foreign funding (Chapter 1);
- provided a stimulus to demand during a period of depression caused by severe terms of trade shocks and previous poor economic policies (Chapter 3);
- made the macroeconomic adjustment program more politically viable (Chapters 2 and 3);
- provided a workable channel for funneling large quantities of foreign and central government funds to many small projects implemented by decentralized agencies, especially municipalities and NGOs (Chapters 1 and 6);
- strengthened some of the institutions with which it worked (Chapters 3 and 6);
- helped establish government/NGO relations (Chapter 6);
- strengthened the democratic process by giving many people and organizations a sense that for the first time ever, the government had done something for their benefit (Chapter 3); and
- provided the impetus to the World Bank and other agencies to experiment with new kinds of projects concerned with the social costs of economic crises and adjustment (Chapter 2).

The ESF's Shortcomings

Although the ESF did many things well, it fell well short of perfection, or even best practice, in a number of areas. Most of its deficiencies were foreseen (or, in retrospect, foreseeable) and acceptable consequences of the ESF's "emergency" mandate to act as quickly as possible in the face of the country's economic crisis. The ESF's short start-up period, the quick turn-around of project proposals, its low administrative overhead, and the demand-driven approach to project generation were all deliberate design measures that involved trade-offs. Targeting, project selection, and project sustainability were three of the most important areas where quality was sacrificed in favor of quantity and speed.

Key areas in which the ESF either was never, from the outset, intended to have an impact, or where it fell short of its own goals, included the following:

- The ESF did not solve Bolivia's unemployment problems (Chapters 3 and 4).
- The ESF did not substantially address unemployment created specifically by the adjustment program, i.e., the laid-off employees of the state mining company (Chapter 4).
- The ESF did not, in most cases, reach the poorest of the poor (Chapters 3, 4 and 9).
- The project selection process was not sufficiently rigorous to guarantee that only the best projects were picked. Indeed some projects financed did not meet minimum social return criteria (Chapters 3, 7 and 9).
- The appraisal and supervision process allowed some works of inadequate quality to slip through (Chapter 3).

- The limited integration with the national and regional planning processes led, in some cases, to inefficient investments (Chapters 8 and 9).
- Inadequate provisions for operations and maintenance after ESF financing expires may shorten the useful life of the infrastructure created (Chapters 8 and 9).

Key Ingredients for Success[1]

The key conditions for the relative success of the ESF were:

- *The ESF was given strong protection from political interference.* President Paz Estenssoro's personal commitment and the mechanisms of the governing coalition ensured freedom from petty party politics. The ESF was thus able to hire its staff and appraise projects on strictly technical grounds.
- *The ESF learned by doing.* As problems or bottlenecks arose, the ESF adjusted its staffing, structure and procedures to overcome them.
- *The ESF was organized as a financial intermediary,* rather than as a direct employer or project-implementing agency. Projects originated from other institutions or in the beneficiary community, were managed by them, and used small private contractors to implement the work. This created important incentives and disciplines that would otherwise have been absent.
- *The ESF focused on small-scale, technologically simple projects.* This allowed targeting by type of project, enabled communities and local organizations to design and implement projects, and decreased the cost of maintenance.
- *Its staff was of the highest caliber.* They were exceptionally capable, hardworking, and honest. This was accomplished by dynamic leadership providing a results-oriented, non-bureaucratic work environment, and by paying private sector salaries.
- *Unconventional procurement procedures were used.* Most of the works financed were small and simple enough to lend themselves to the use of uniform unit prices.
- *The ESF developed an effective management information system.* It would have been impossible to keep track of the volume of transactions without it. It also greatly enhanced the transparency of the fund's operations, thereby reinforcing honesty, and gaining donor confidence.
- *The ESF's accountability mechanisms* helped keep it "honest" without taking away operational flexibility. The ESF had to answer regularly to the president, the Congress and the press. Moreover, the ESF's reliance on local agencies meant that it was held accountable by them.
- *The ESF managed its donors well.* The ESF did not allow donors to design their own programs. Rather the donors agreed to the ESF's procedures as a whole. Donors' funds were then disbursed against the ESF's overall portfolio, or to certain categories of projects therein.

- *The ESF worked with both governmental and private institutions.* This fostered a healthy competition that exploited the comparative advantages of each type of institution.
- *The ESF's temporary status* made it possible to exempt it from standard civil service rules, and limited problems of rivalry with other government institutions.
- *The ESF's philosophy was consistent with the macroeconomic framework.* The adjustment program sought to increase the role of the private sector in the economy. The private sector orientation of the ESF is demonstrated in its focus on basic infrastructure and social services; its payment of market wages; its use of private contractors; and its use of decentralized agencies to formulate and implement projects.

Is the ESF replicable? Many of the key ingredients in the ESF's success are replicable: its management information system, project appraisal procedures, accountability mechanisms, donor management, etc., can be replicated or improved upon by other countries. Its more ephemeral ingredients: protection from political interference, dynamic leadership, excellent staff and institutional flexibility were also key ingredients and may be more difficult to reproduce.

Notes

1. We are indebted to Graham Smith of the World Bank for first systematizing the ingredients for success.

Bibliography

Castaños, María Inés, *et al.* "Evaluación de las Acciones y Proyectos del Fondo Social de Emergencia." Mimeo. La Paz, Bolivia, 1988.

CEDLA. "Informe Final de la Evaluación Acerca del Impacto Social de los Proyectos del Fondo Social de Emergencia en la Ciudad de el Alto." Mimeo. La Paz, Bolivia, November 1989.

Edirisinghe, Neville. *The Food Stamp Scheme in Sri Lanka: Costs, Benefits, and Options for Modification.* Research Report No. 58. Washington, D.C.: International Food Policy Research Institute, 1987.

Graham, Carol. "The Politics of the Bolivian Emergency Social Fund." Mimeo. Washington, D.C.: Brookings Institution, 1991.

Grosh, Margaret E. "The Jamaican Food Stamps Program: A Case Study." Mimeo. Washington, D.C.: World Bank, 1990a.

———. *Social Spending in Latin America: The Story of the 1980s.* World Bank Discussion Paper No. 106. Washington, D.C.: World Bank, 1990b.

———. "What Should Social Funds Finance?: Portfolio Mix, Targeting, and Efficiency Criteria." View for LATHR No. 3. Washington, D.C.: World Bank, 1990c.

Herrick, Bruce. "Ex-Post Project Evaluation: Emergency Social Fund, Bolivia." Mimeo. Washington, D.C., August 15, 1989.

Molino Rivera, Ramiro, *et. al.* "Proyecto de Promoción e Investigación del Fondo Social de Emergencia: Reporte Final." Mimeo. La Paz, Bolivia, 1988.

Newman, John, Steen Jorgensen, and Menno Pradhan. "How Did Workers Benefit from Bolivia's Emergency Social Fund?" *World Bank Economic Review*, Vol. 5, No. 2, May 1991.

Patiño, Fernando, *et. al.* "Informe Final: Conclusiones y Recomendaciones de la Fiscalia en Salud." Mimeo. La Paz, Bolivia: Emergency Social Fund.

Ravallion, Martin. "Reaching the Rural Poor through Public Employment: Arguments, Evidence, and Lessons from South Asia." *The World Bank Research Observer* Vol. 6, No. 2.

SYSTEMA. "Impacto Institucional del Fondo Social de Emergencia." Mimeo. La Paz, Bolivia, 1989.

Unidad de Analisis de Politica Economica (UDAPE). "Evaluación Macroeconómica del Programa de Inversión: Ejecutado por el Fondo Social de Emergencia 1987-Julio 1989." Mimeo. La Paz, Bolivia, 1989.

———. "Modelo para Medir el Impacto Macro-económico de los Proyectos del Fondo Social de Emergencia." Mimeo. La Paz, Bolivia, 1989.

VanDomelen, Julie. "Geographical Targeting of Poverty by the Emergency Social Fund." Mimeo. La Paz, Bolivia, 1989.

World Bank. *Annual Report 1988*. Washington, D.C.: World Bank, 1988.

———. *Annual Report 1990*. Washington, D.C.: World Bank, 1990.

About the Authors

Mary Barton is project coordinator for the Social Recovery Project in Zambia's Ministry of Finance and National Commission for Development Planning. She was involved over an 18 month period in the daily supervision of the ESF project working as a consultant in the World Bank's Latin American Department III.

Margaret E. Grosh is an economist with the World Bank's Latin America and Caribbean Technical Department, Human Resources Division. She was involved in the very early stages of the Bank's support to the ESF and again in the later implementation phases. She is presently involved in several of the other Latin American Social Fund operations and is an evaluation and monitoring specialist.

Steen Lau Jorgensen is an economist with the World Bank's Southern Africa Department, Population and Human Resources Division. He managed the implementation of the Bank's two credits in support of the ESF from 1987 to 1990 as country officer for Bolivia.

Katherine Marshall is Director of the World Bank's Sahelian Department in the Africa Region. She was division chief in the Country Operations Division for Bolivia from 1985 to 1990 and managed the work on both the macroeconomic adjustment program and the ESF.

John L. Newman is an economist in the Welfare and Human Resources Division of the World Bank's Population and Human Resources Department. He was involved in the monitoring of ESF activities through various household surveys.

Menno Pradhan was a research assistant in the Welfare and Human Resources Division of the World Bank's Population and Human Resource Department, and is now at Tilberg University, the Netherlands.

Mark Schacter is a consultant with the World Bank's Poverty and Social Policy Division in the Technical Department for the Africa Region. He worked as a consultant on the dissemination of the ESF experience.

Graham Smith is the Chief of the Infrastructure and Energy Division in the Latin America and Caribbean Department III of the World Bank. He managed appraisal of the World Bank's two credits in support of the ESF.

Constance Sepeda is a Senior Project Officer in the Bank's Human Resources Division, Latin America and Caribbean Department III, and is responsible for the Bank's support to the successor of the ESF, the Social Investment Fund.

Julie VanDomelen is an economist with the World Bank and was a consultant with the World Bank's Resident Mission in Bolivia, where she was closely involved in the daily supervision of ESF activities from 1988 to its closure.